The Jews in Western Europe
1400–1600

As European politics, society, economy and religion underwent epoch-making changes between 1400 and 1600, the treatment of Europe's Jews by the non-Jewish majority was, then as in later periods, a symptom of social problems and tensions in the Continent as a whole.

Through a broad-ranging collection of documents, John Edwards sets out to present a vivid picture of the Jewish presence in European life during this vital and turbulent period. Subjects covered include the Jews' own economic presence and culture, social relations between Jews and Christians, and the policies and actions of Christian authorities in Church and State. He also draws upon original source material to convey ordinary people's prejudices about Jews, including myths about Jewish 'devilishness', moneygrabbing, and 'ritual murder' of Christian children.

Full introductory and explanatory material makes accessible the historical context of the subject and highlights the insights offered by the documents as well as the pitfalls to be avoided in this area of historical enquiry.

Manchester Medieval Sources Series

series adviser Janet L. Nelson

This series aims to meet a growing need amongst students and teachers of medieval history for translations of key sources that are directly usable in students' own work. The series will provide texts central to medieval studies courses and will focus upon the diverse cultural, social as well as political conditions that affected the functioning of all levels of medieval society. The basic premise of the new series is that translations must be accompanied by sufficient introductory and explanatory material and each volume will therefore include a comprehensive guide to the sources' interpretation, including discussion of critical linguistic problems and an assessment of the most recent research on the topics being covered.

already published in the series

Janet L. Nelson *The Annals of St-Bertin: ninth-century histories, volume I*

Timothy Reuter *The Annals of Fulda: ninth-century histories, volume II*

Chris Given-Wilson *Chronicles of the Revolution, 1397–1400: the reign of Richard II*

R. N. Swanson *Catholic England: faith, religion and observance before the Reformation*

Rosemary Horrox *The Black Death*

forthcoming titles in the series will include

Donald Bullough *The Vikings in Paris*

Simon Lloyd *The impact of the crusades: the experience of England, 1095–1274*

Richard Smith *Sources for the population history of England, 1000–1540*

J. A. Watt *The origins of anti-semitism in Europe*

Alison McHardy *The early reign of Richard II*

Ian Robinson *The pontificate of Gregory VII*

Edward Powell *Crime, law and society in late medieval England*

Jeremy Goldberg *Women in England*

THE JEWS
IN WESTERN EUROPE
1400–1600

translated and edited by John Edwards

Manchester University Press
Manchester and New York

distributed exclusively in the USA and Canada by St. Martin's Press

Copyright © John Edwards 1994

Published by Manchester University Press
Oxford Road, Manchester M13 9NR, UK
and Room 400, 175 Fifth Avenue, New York, NY 10010, USA

Distributed exclusively in the USA and Canada
by St. Martin's Press, Inc., 175 Fifth Avenue, New York, NY 10010, USA

British Library Cataloguing-in-Publication Data
A catalogue record for this book is available from the British Library

Library of Congress Cataloging-in-Publication Data
The Jews in Western Europe / translated and edited by John Edwards.
        p.   cm. — (Manchester medieval sources series)
    Translation of documents originally written in Latin, Hebrew,
French, German, Portuguese, Spanish and Italian
    Includes bibliographical references and index.
    ISBN 0-7190-3508-2. — ISBN 0-7190-3509-0 (pbk.)
        1. Jews—Europe—History—Sources. 2. Judaism—Relations—
Christianity—History—Sources. 3. Christianity and other
religions—History—Sources. 4. Jews—History—70-1789—Sources.
5. Europe—Ethnic relations—Sources. I. Edwards, John, 1949-.
II. Series.
DS135.E81J48   1995
940'.04924—dc20   94-11584

ISBN 0 7190 3508 2 *hardback*
ISBN 0 7190 3509 0 *paperback*

Typeset in Monotype Bell
by Koinonia Ltd, Manchester
Printed in Great Britain
by Bell & Bain Ltd, Glasgow

Contents

For Viv

*'Set me like a seal on your heart, like a seal on your arm.
For love is strong as death.'*

[Song of Songs 8:6]

Foreword

Attentive to the nuances of language, and hence the hazards of translation, John Edwards presents here a selection of the documentary sources for Christian intellectual attitudes towards, and Christians' relations with, Jews in their midst, during the fifteenth and sixteenth centuries. Here are exposed the ideological roots of a medieval mentality which persisted through and beyond the Reformation and Counter-Reformation. Drawing extensively on archival materials, and especially those of Mediterranean western Europe, John Edwards presents rich evidence for the distinctive economic activities of Jews within Christian societies. He shows the varieties of Jewish responses both to the opportunities of urban life, and to the fundamental insecurities of their own position as they attempted to appease and pre-empt Christian persecution at central and local levels. Through these texts readers will be able to reconstruct complex and volatile relationships between Jews and Christians, to discern practice often at odds with official prescription, and to trace the beliefs that legitimised the expulsion of Jews from Christian states. John Edwards' coverage of late medieval and early modern Europe shows crucial continuities linking periods often, and misleadingly, treated apart. His book admirably fulfils the aims of the MUP series. It constitutes an original and masterly contribution to the history of European Jewry and so to that of Europe itself.

Janet L. Nelson, King's College London

Preface

In 1988, I published a work entitled *The Jews in Christian Europe, 1400-1700*[1], which aimed at 'a two-way view of Christian and Jewish life, with a stress on the relationships between adherents of the two faiths, rather than on their separate and internal histories'.[2] Inevitably, this was not entirely possible in a short monograph, but the invitation to contribute to the present series provides an opportunity to add one vital dimension to the earlier work, that is, the presentation of original documentary sources from the period concerned. Although many scholars have laboured to make such material available to a general readership, their efforts have, up to now, been scattered among various learned works. What has so far been lacking, as I have discovered during ten years' teaching of an undergraduate course in medieval and, latterly, early modern Jewish history in the University of Birmingham, has been a convenient selection of documentary sources which might form the basis of such a course. The present work attempts to respond to that need.

The history and background of the Jewish presence in fifteenth- and sixteenth-century Europe is discussed in the Introduction which follows, but it is necessary to state at the outset that the selection of texts which is offered here is inevitably just a small and arbitrary sample of the sources which are available. By the very nature of the surviving documents, a certain imbalance towards the Christian 'side' is unavoidable. History tends to be written by majorities and 'winners' rather than minorities and 'losers'. It may also be observed that there is a certain weighting in favour of Southern European sources, and particularly those of Spain and Italy, in the selection of sources offered here. This matter will be discussed in the Introduction. At this stage, though, it is necessary only to note that the primary purpose of this collection of sources is to provide a working translation for the use of students of general, religious and Jewish history, and to help the general reader also to gain a better and more colourful picture of how Jews and Christians lived in Europe in this period, and how they did, or did not, get on together. The problems and pitfalls of the process

1 London, 1988; revised, paperback edition, 1991.
2 John Edwards, *The Jews in Christian Europe*, 1991 edn, p. ix.

of translation itself are discussed in the Note on the documents.

Finally, as is the convention, acknowledgements are in order. I would like to thank all my colleagues in the School of History in the University of Birmingham for their comradeship and scholarship during most of the last two decades. In particular, I wish to thank Robert Swanson, who has also contributed to the present series, for his example in trimming this work to a proper shape, even though he has not yet read a word of it! I am also grateful to Jane Thorniley-Walker for being such a kind and understanding editor, even when externally-imposed and unforeseen difficulties so often delayed the completion of this book, and to Michelle O'Connell, who took over in the latter stages of production. I must also thank my Birmingham students, who, probably without knowing it, have given me so much inspiration and courage over the years, and who have stoically accepted the imposition of earlier drafts of some of what follows. My greatest debt of all, though, is recorded in the dedication

Moseley, Birmingham,
on the Feast of St Mary Magdalen, 1993.

Note on the documents

Translators belong to a class of professionals whom the world takes pleasure in reviling. Like estate agents, auditors and accountants, they enjoy a function similar to that performed by the sin-eaters of certain primitive communities, whose job was to absorb others' sense of wrongdoing through the consumption of a ritual meal. Should we fail to enjoy, let alone understand, a novel or a poem, we can always lay the guilt on a faulty rendering, with a swipe or two at syntax and vocabulary for good measure.[1]

In writing these words, Jonathan Keates was reviewing the recent reprint of George Steiner's great study of translation and the translator's art, *After Babel*.[2] His opening salvo does little to inspire with joy and optimism one who is about to present to the reader, in translation, a complex set of sources for the history of western and central European Jews in the fifteenth and sixteenth centuries.

The selection of documents which is presented here was originally written in a wide range of languages – Latin, Hebrew, French, German, Portuguese, Spanish and Italian. All these languages were spoken, or at least understood, by fifteenth- and sixteenth-century Europeans, in various countries, whether they were Jews or Christians – or, in the case of Spain, Muslims. It may be thought that, when it comes to 'historical' as opposed to 'literary' texts, there is no need for the translator to agonise over the problem raised by Keates. The author of the work he reviewed had, however very different ideas on the subject.

Steiner wrote, in a passage he describes as a 'truism', that 'Translation exists because men speak different languages'.[3] His expressed purpose in composing the chapter which precedes this observation was to demonstrate that, since linguistic chaos exists in the world, and has done, in metaphor at least, ever since the building of the tower of **Babel** [see Glossary], all communications, even within the expression of a single human 'language', require an exercise in decoding. Such observations clearly apply at least as much to 'historical documents' as they do to the literary texts which normally exercise the professional translator and his or her readership.

1 Jonathan Keates in *The Independent*, 8 May 1993.
2 George Steiner, *After Babel. Aspects of language and translation*, Oxford, 1975, 1993.
3 Steiner, *After Babel*, 1975 edn, p. 49.

Because of the centrality of Judæo-Christian experience in the life and history of Europeans, in the fifteenth and sixteenth centuries and since, and particularly because both these religions so much revere their written texts, or 'Scriptures', on which faith and practice are meant to be based, questions of translation or 'decoding' must be considered in relation to what follows. In view of this it is hardly surprising that it was in the case of translations of the Bible that Europeans first confronted these issues, and did so precisely in the period which is covered by the present work. In an essay on English translations of the Bible, Gerald Hammond tackled the problems which face all those who attempt to render a text into another language, including those others whose translations have, in certain cases, been used here. In general terms, he notes that '"Translation" is one of the most influential forms of literary criticism, for it both interprets and creates the text it addresses. Indeed, in its original uses in English, the word *interpret* means "translate".' He also observes, in this essay, that 'Idioms are even more embedded in language and culture systems than single words are, so that what is offered is not translation but only an equivalent'.[4] By way of illustration Hammond recounts some episodes in the controversy, which took place in the 1520s – and 1530s, between two famous English Christian figures, Thomas More, who died as a Catholic because of his refusal to recognise King Henry VIII's supremacy over the Church in England, and William Tyndale, who became an inspiration to Protestants. The issue was the latter's English translation of the Christian New Testament. Tyndale's responses to More's challenges over particular renderings indicate that translators in that period were little troubled by that 'semantic accuracy' which Hammond rightly describes as an illusion.[5] The point at issue here, though, is nothing less than the very nature of the translations which follow. If historical documents are indeed to be treated with the care and attention normally lavished on what is commonly called 'literature' – novels, poetry, plays, and so on – then the question of 'accuracy' must be addressed from the outset.

In essence, there seem to be two main approaches to translation. In the first case, one can attempt a 'literal' rendering of the text in hand. This means that the translator should follow, as far as possible, the style and phraseology of the original document, even if they do not convert

4 Gerald Hammond, 'English translations of the Bible', in *The literary guide to the Bible*, eds Robert Alter and Frank Kermode, London, 1987, p. 649.

5 Hammond, 'English translations', pp. 651-2.

easily into English expression. The alternative approach is the attempt to produce a translation which does 'read well' in English, even if this means that sentences have to be re-arranged, and forms of expression changed. An illustration of the problems which arise from the need to resolve this issue comes from sixteenth-century debate over the way in which the Holy Scriptures themselves should be translated.

In the thirteenth chapter of Paul's First Letter to the Corinthians, there is a famous passage in which the author describes, to the members of that church, what he saw to be the proper nature of Christian behaviour. The main subject of the earlier verses of this chapter, in the original Greek, *agape*, is commonly translated either as 'love' or as 'charity'. In his translation, Tyndale uses 'love', but More regarded this as a dangerously 'untheological' word. For him, 'charity' was safer, because it more closely resembled the expression used in the Latin translation, the Vulgate [see document 1 below], which was the version commonly used by the Western Church at the time. The Latin word used here was *c[h]aritas*. The point is that both men came to the Biblical text with their own purposes and prejudices. More was desperate to preserve the Catholic Church which he knew and loved, and of which the Vulgate (even though it was known by the 1520s to be based on an inadequate range of texts and to contain 'inaccuracies') was a bastion, while Tyndale believed that the Bible should be freed of deliberate Catholic obstruction, which largely kept it in the hands of the clergy and of the better-educated among the laity, and be given directly to all the Christian people of England. Thus their respective uses of the texts of Scripture were developed under the influence, not only of a desire to render the Biblical text accurately, but also of their individual hopes and fears for the future of the Western Church.

This is just one example of the general truth that all translation depends, not only on the skill and accuracy of the translator, but also on his or her background and approach to the task. However, the effect and effectiveness of a translation also depend on the skill and background of the reader.[6] Each word is like a package of associations and memories, which speaks differently to each person, and yet an inner core of 'accuracy', in the sense of a common Judæo-Christian history and heritage, exists throughout. It would be unduly presumptuous to suggest that a happy balance between literal accuracy and lively interpretation has been achieved in the translations which follow [at

6 The General Introduction and the Bibliography of Printed Works Cited are intended to help the reader in this respect.

least those for which the present author is responsible], but the varied registers of language which are used in these texts are intended to do as much as possible to convey what appears to be the sense of the original. This means that the English versions offered here must attempt to reflect, for example, the language of Papal lawyers, or else that of government draughtsmen, or of private citizens making personal and business arrangements, or of preachers, theologians, novelists and poets. Many of these texts are clearly the work of one author, who is named, but the various ecclesiastical and secular legal documents, which are included in the collection, do not have undisputed authorship. Yet, if 'historical' documents are indeed to be treated as what they in fact are, that is, 'literary' texts, then the problem of authorship, which has so vexed scholars and critics in recent years,[7] must be addressed, if a suitable kind of language is to be used to translate them.

None of these documents is straightforward. As I wrote some years ago,

> It must be evident, at the most basic level, to both the historian and the literary scholar, that even the most common words, such as *rey* [king] or *señorío* [lordship] are not immutable in meaning, and have to be considered not only in their textual uses, but also in the circumstances in which the texts which employ them were produced.[8]

Nowhere are these words more applicable than to the religious vocabulary, with its diverse Jewish and Christian understandings and interpretations, which fills so many of these documents. As for their historical context, the General Introduction and the shorter introductions to the chapters, attempt to address the matter. The reader should, however, bear in mind throughout George Steiner's warning.

> The historian's problem as to what he is talking about is a genuine one. He must not only 'explain' his document, i.e. paraphrase, transcribe, gloss it at the lexical-grammatical level, but also 'understand' it, i.e. show '*how* what was said was meant and thus what *relations* there may have been between various different statements within the same general context'. And the meaning thus arrived at must be the 'true one'. By what metamorphic magic is the historian to proceed?[9]

7 See, for example, Ann Jefferson and David Robey, *Modern literary theory. A comparative introduction* (London, 1982).

8 John Edwards, '*Conversos*, Judaism and the language of monarchy in fifteenth-century Castile', in *Circa 1492. Proceedings of the Jerusalem Colloquium: Litteræ Judæorum in Terra Hispanica* [1984], ed. Isaac Benabu (Jerusalem, 1992 [1993]), p. 209.

9 Steiner, *After Babel*, pp. 135-6, including a quotation from Quentin Skinner, 'Meaning and understanding in the history of ideas', *History and Theory*, vii (1969), p. 47.

To turn to more mundane matters, a glossary is provided, to help with some of the more specialised vocabulary which has to be used. The first use in the text of each of the terms included in the glossary is marked by the use of **bold** type. Also, where translated passages involve cuts or omissions from the full text, the usual symbol, '…', is included and, where explanatory material has been inserted into the text, it has been placed in square brackets. The wide range of languages in which these documents originated, together with the diversity of the countries and regions to which they refer, inevitably raises, for the translator, the problem of how to render personal and place names. The general principle followed here has been to use English versions of placenames where they exist, leaving the rest in the original. As is common in historical writing, personal names have also normally been left in their original form, but rulers' names have been anglicised where possible and appropriate.

It is hoped that the words of these texts have been 'unpacked' sufficiently to allow at least some of the experience of Jews and Christians in fifteenth- and sixteenth-century Europe to be conveyed to those with experience of another and later century.

Acknowledgements

The author wishes to acknowledge the following copyright-holders:

Extracts from
- the Jerusalem Bible: Darton, Longman & Todd
- the Vulgate Bible: EDICA S.A., Madrid (Biblioteca de Autores Cristianos)

Other extracts listed by document number
3A: Sociéte d'Editions 'les Belles Lettres', Paris
3B: Ecole Practique des Hautes Etudes, Paris, and Mouton et Cie, Paris and the Hague
4A & B: The Regents of the University of California
4C: Editions Galilée, Paris
5A: Magnes Press, Hebrew University of Jerusalem
7, 9, 21, 29B, 30, 35C, 38, 40B, 44A and B, 45, 47: Pontifical Institute of Medieval
    Studies, Toronto
11: Author and Institución Fernando el Católico, Zaragoza
19: Magnes Press, Hebrew University of Jerusalem
29A, 46: Nischi-Lischi, Pisa
34: Brill, Leiden
40C: Abaris Books, New York
41A and B: Fortress Press, Philadelphia
43: Yale University
48: Clásicos Castalia, Madrid
49: Princeton University Press

Copyright in the following belongs to their respective authors: documents 5B, 17, 20, 24B, 31B, 37A and B.

General introduction: Jews as Europeans in the fifteenth and sixteenth centuries

The Jewish contribution to European history

Most of world history until the later eighteenth century could be written without more than marginal references to the Jews, except as a small people which pioneered the monotheistic world religions, a debt acknowledged by Islam, but creating endless problems for Christianity, or rather for the Jews unlucky enough to live under Christian rulers. Practically the entire intellectual history of the Western world, and all that of the great cultures of the East, could be written without more than a few footnotes about the direct Jewish contribution to them, though not without paying considerable attention to the role of Jews as intermediaries and cultural brokers, notably between the Classic Mediterranean heritage, Islam and the medieval West. This is rather surprising when we consider the extraordinary prominence in twentieth century cultural, intellectual and public life of members of this small people which, even at its demographic peak before the Holocaust, formed less than one per cent of the world's population.

Since most of public life was closed to them, their absence from it before the French Revolution was perhaps to be expected.... With the possible exception of medicine, where the acknowledged Jewish expertise crossed communal frontiers, Jewish learning and intellectual effort focused on holy matters.[1]

The instinct of most people would probably be to agree with this distinguished historian's assessment of the Jewish contribution to the history of Europe. Indeed, until quite recently, it would have been fairly hard to do otherwise, given the poor availability of material to indicate the contrary.

Two main matters must be tackled at the outset and the first of them is clearly delineated in Hobsbawm's comments. Up to now it has been not only possible, but indeed normal, for the history of the late medieval and early modern periods to be written without any regard for the Continent's Jewish inhabitants. Remarks, written some years ago about Poland and before the recent political changes there, could,

1 E. J. Hobsbawm, in the *London Review of Books*, XV, no. 7 [8 April 1993], p. 20, reviewing Peter Pulzer, *Jews and the German state: the political history of a minority, 1848-1933*, Oxford, 1992, and Ruth Gay, *The Jews of Germany: a historical portrait*, New Haven and London, 1992.

with appropriate adjustments, equally well describe the situation in many countries further west.

> It is perhaps in modern Polish historians ... that the uneasiness of those who experienced, or have subsequently to contemplate, the history of that country becomes most apparent.... Whatever the political and historical viewpoint of the writer, the Jews seem to be something of an embarrass- ment to the non-Jew. There seems to be an underlying feeling that they have been badly treated, but that to indicate this clearly is to admit something which threatens to destroy whatever self-respect and independ- ence, at least of mind, remain to a proud but much-abused people.[2]

A recent historian of eighteenth-century Poland has written,

> To all intents and purposes, the Jews formed a separate estate inside the Commonwealth [of Poland and Lithuania]. Their communities, the cahals, centred round the synagogue, to which might be attached a school, a communal bakery, printing shop or bathhouse. In a narrower sense, the cahal was the council of elders and rabbis, who provided administration and justice. They ran their own courts, they apportioned the state poll-tax and levied their own dues and taxes. They decided whether or not to confer the *chazaka*, citizenship, on newcomers, essential if they were to be accepted into the community. They could also expel and ruin fellow Jews by excommunication, *herem*. The Christian municipal authorities had no say in such matters.[3]

It will be interesting to see, from the documents which follow, how far such observations apply to an earlier period and to more westerly countries. In any case though, it seems that this general sense of unease, separation and even alienation between Jew and Gentile has only been increased by the horrors of the twentieth century, of which Europe's Jews have been leading victims. It is now hard for most people, though evidently not all, to see the Continent's history in terms of its inevitable 'progress' towards higher civilisation and [self-] righteous world domination. Nonetheless, it would be hard to find anyone who would deny the importance of the Renaissance and the Reformation, with the succeeding Counter-Reformation, which are assumed to have led to the development of the European economy and of what is still commonly termed the 'modern' world. Thus for many, the 'received wisdom' still is that many of the supposedly beneficent

2 John Edwards, *The Jews in Christian Europe, 1400-1700*, London, 1988, 1991, p. 115 [this and later references are to the revised, 1991 edition].

3 Jerzy Lukowski, *Liberty's folly. The Polish-Lithuanian Commonwealth in the eighteenth century*, London, 1991, pp. 78-9.

developments in more recent history originated in the period covered by this book, that is to say, the fifteenth and sixteenth centuries. Where, then, were Europe's Jews, while these momentous events were unfolding? It is hoped that the collection of texts which follows will provide some kind of answer to that question.

It has to be noted that this particular vision of history contains certain paradoxes for those who have some regard for that concept which is still quite commonly referred to as the 'Christian West'. After all, how did that 'civilisation' originate and why was it called 'Christian' in the first place? At this point, it is necessary to go back in time and look at two phenomena which crucially influenced Jewish history in the period between 1400 and 1600, that is to say, the settlement of Jews in Western Europe and the rise and spread of Christianity.

Jewish settlement and expulsion

Before its collapse in the fifth century, Jews seem to have lived in nearly all the provinces of the western Roman empire, with particularly prominent settlements in Italy itself, Spain, Gaul and what is now Germany. Thus in many of the areas covered by the documents in this book, Jews had lived continuously from the beginning of the Christian era until the late Middle Ages. This was certainly so in Spain, southern France (as Gaul had become) and Italy. Both the 'Barbarian' successor states of the West and the Catholic Church inherited late Roman legislation concerning Jews as well as so many other subjects.[4] Thus, by the end of the fourteenth century, a Jewish minority was quite widely spread over much of Western and Central Europe. Between the fifth century and the starting-point of this documentary selection, Jews had lived, either continuously or temporarily, in England, France, the Iberian peninsula, Italy and the German and other Central European territories which had come to be known as the 'Holy Roman Empire'. There is no significant evidence of Jewish settlement in the rest of the British Isles, in Scandinavia, or the Low Countries. The overall continuity of Jewish settlement in the western half of the European continent in the early and High Middle Ages does not, however, indicate that Jews could necessarily rely on security or permanence.

4 For a useful survey of the Spanish case, in which the seventh-century Visigothic monarchy legislated in an increasingly severe manner against Jews, until such efforts were overwhelmed by the Muslim invasion of 711-713, see Roger Collins, *Early medieval Spain. Unity in diversity, 400–1000*, London, 1983, pp. 129-42.

For Jews, the period covered by the present work was dominated by the phenomenon of expulsion, or, as it would apparently be described today, 'ethnic cleansing'. As the documents offered below will clearly indicate, the main examples of mass, or 'national' expulsion took place in Spain in 1492 and Portugal in 1497. However, the other, more local, examples of such a policy, which are included in chapter 2 [documents 21 and 22], are no more than particular reflections of a much more widespread tendency which could probably, for reasons which will be suggested below, be termed a movement, even though there was no direct co-ordination between the authorities who implemented, or attempted to implement, such measures. In any case, the result of the events of the late Middle Ages, from the thirteenth century up to about 1500, was that a well-established Jewish presence disappeared from large areas of Western Europe.

The process began with Edward I of England's expulsion of the Jews of his Gascon territories in south-western France, in 1288, and of the entire English community of Jews in 1290. Between 1306 and 1394, the Capetian and Valois rulers of France made a series of attempts to remove Jews from the territories under their control, while the devastations of the bubonic plague, which is commonly known as the 'Black Death', both during its original outbreak in 1348-1351 and its subsequent recurrences well into the next century, led to further local attacks on Jewish communities. As a result there were further local expulsions in Germany, and further attempts at such measures in France and Spain [for the latter, see document 9]. Apart from the case of England, though, permanent or at least long-term expulsions only began effectively in the fifteenth century, first in Germany and Austria, for example in Vienna in 1421, Cologne in 1424, Augsburg in 1439, all of Bavaria in 1442 (with a second attempt in 1450), and the royal towns in Moravia in 1454. Fragmented politics led to the continuation of this piecemeal approach in the Empire, and the result was that, by 1510, Jews had additionally been largely or completely removed from Geneva (by then part of the Swiss Confederation), Mecklenburg, Pomerania, Halle, Magdeburg, Lower Austria, Styria, Carinthia, Württemberg, the archdiocese of Salzburg, Nuremberg, Ulm, and Brandenburg. By the time that Brother Martin Luther posted his famous ninety-five theses on the door of Wittenberg church in 1517, there were no Jews living, legally, at least, in England, in France, apart from a few small papal territories in the southeast, in the Spanish kingdoms and Portugal, or in most of the rest of North-western and

Central Europe. Indeed, by 1500, it appeared that a similar process was under way in Italy, a country which had a similarly fragmented political geography. Jews were officially expelled from Perugia in 1485, Vicenza in 1486, Parma in 1488, Milan and Lucca a year later, and Florence (as a result of the French invasion) in 1494. Ferdinand and Isabella extended the provisions of their 1492 expulsion edict [document 10] to Sardinia and Sicily, in the same year, and when Ferdinand and his Spanish troops took control of the kingdom of Naples from the French in 1510, they attempted to implement a similar policy in much of southern Italy. Meanwhile, the advancing Valois French monarchy had, in 1498, ordered the departure of Jews from Provence (to the east of the Rhône, but not, of course, including Papal territory). It thus appeared, by the second decade of the sixteenth century, that the centre of gravity of European Jewish life had moved irrevocably eastwards, with Poland and Lithuania taking over from Iberia as the main demographic, cultural and religious centre of Judaism. Events in the latter part of the sixteenth century, and in the decades after 1600, were to demonstrate that such a view would not be totally accurate. Nonetheless, it is true that most of the Jews who remained in Western Europe after 1500, in southern France, Germany and Italy, lived under the rule of the Church, whether of the Popes or of their subordinates.[5] Thus it is now time to address the question of the Church's policy towards the Jews in this period, in both theological and practical terms.

The Church and the Jews

It could be argued that the very nature of medieval, and indeed of later, Christianity was determined by the need of the younger faith to define itself against the older. This is not the place for a detailed discussion of the composition of the various texts which came to form the 'New Testament' of the Christian Bible, but it is hard to deny that one of the underlying themes of these texts is an exaltation of the role of Christ and of his Church, which inevitably implied the downgrading of the Jewish faith and practice in which Jesus and his disciples were brought up. From the very beginning of Mark's gospel, which is generally held to be the earliest, the message is clear. After announcing what is in effect the title of his work, the writer immediately goes on to quote one of the Jewish prophets:

5 Edward, *The Jews in Christian Europe*, pp. 11-12; W. C. Jordan, *The French monarchy and the Jews, From Philip Augustus to the last Capetians*, Philadelphia, 1989; Jonathan Israel, *European Jewry in the age of mercantilism, 1550-1750*, Oxford, 1987, pp. 5-9.

Look, I am going to send my messenger before you; he will prepare your way.[6]

He was, of course, introducing John the Baptist as the precursor of Jesus, but this and all the other texts which became part of the New Testament apparently worked on the assumption that Judaism at the time of Christ was in decline, if not dying, so that only the arrival of the one who proved eventually to be the founder of Christianity, and not just another in the earlier series of Jewish prophets, could save first the Jews and then the rest of the world. Because of the vital importance of the assumptions included in the Christian Biblical texts to the future life and health of Jews who found themselves under Christian rule, including those in late medieval and early modern Europe, some examples from the New Testament texts have been included here [document 1 and introduction to chapter 1]. It is important to remember, though, that most Christians in that period did not read the Bible for themselves. Recent studies have increasingly demonstrated, for example in the case of England, a country which effectively contained no Jews during the fifteenth century and most of the sixteenth, that knowledge of the Scriptures did indeed reach Christian people all over Europe, by various audio-visual means.[7] The crucial point for the purpose of this discussion, is, however, that the interpretation of the 'true' nature of Jews and Judaism was largely kept in the hands of the representatives of the Catholic, or Roman, Church.

The picture which thus emerged was inevitably influenced by the highly negative portrayal of Judaism in the New Testament and in the subsequent commentaries on its texts by the so-called Church 'Fathers', a series of theologians who wrote in Greek and Latin during the late Roman and early medieval periods. It was also influenced by the history of Christianity and in particular by the transformation of the Catholic Church, which then still included both Western and Eastern Orthodox Christians, from a persecuted, minority organisation into the dominant cult of the Roman Empire, after the conversion of the emperor Constantine in the early fourth century.[8] Whatever the

6 The quotation, from Malachi 3:1 [Jerusalem Bible] is run together in Mark 1:3 with one from Isaiah, to whom both are attributed.

7 R. N. Swanson, *Catholic England*, pp. 4–6; Eamon Duffy, *The stripping of the altars. Traditional religion in England, 1400-1580*, New Haven and London, 1992, pp. 53–87.

8 The precise date, if any, of Constantine's conversion cannot be stated, though his departure from paganism (whether or not it was ever complete) seems to have taken place between 312 and 324 [Carsten Peter Thiede, *Heritage of the First Christians. Tracing early Christianity in Europe*, trans., Knut Hein, Oxford, 1992, pp. 124–7].

detailed history of the spread of Christianity in the late Roman Empire may have been, it is undeniable that the newly powerful Catholic Church was able to put its policies into practice as never before, frequently with the full apparatus of the still mighty Roman empire behind it. This was, of course the state which, when still pagan, had persecuted Jews as well as Christians, having tried, by the destruction of the temple at Jerusalem in 70 A.D., to remove the worship of God from the earth altogether.[9] For the medieval Church, and for the Jews of the period, the implications of the 'conversion' of Constantine were to be of immense significance. Medieval popes based their powers, over Christians and Jews, on the supposed gift or 'donation' by Constantine to Pope Sylvester (reigned 314-335) of imperial as well as ecclesiastical power over the Western Catholic Church. This legend was intended by the Franks and their supporters to reduce Lombard control over the Papacy in the later eighth century and increase their own. It was exposed as a forgery as early as the year 1001, by the chancery of the emperor Otto III, and was to be denounced once again by a papal secretary of a later vintage, Lorenzo Valla, during the pontificate of Nicholas V (1447-1455).[10] Nonetheless, it was to have its effect on Christian treatment of medieval Jews in one important respect. It helped to establish a clear correlation between religious and social power.

The New Testament and the Jews

Here again, the origins of the Papacy's notion of Christian society, and how it and its Jewish minority were to be governed, were to have considerable implications for European Jews in the fifteenth and sixteenth centuries. The relevant New Testament texts were, as so often, ambivalent, and it is important always to remember that Catholics in this period used the Latin 'Vulgate' translation, so that later readings, which may be more accurate, are not relevant to this discussion [Note on the Documents, p.xiv, and document 1]. Thus, while some of the recorded words of Jesus seem to imply that he was not interested in worldly affairs and that his followers should avoid such entanglements too, others imply the necessity for conflict in the establishment of the hoped-for kingdom of God, and a worldwide mission to bring all human beings into that kingdom.

9 John Gager, *The origins of anti-Semitism*, New York, 1983.

10 Walter Ullmann, *A short history of the Papacy in the Middle Ages*, London, 1972, pp. 77-80; Malcolm Barber, *The two cities. Medieval Europe, 1050-1320*, London, 1992, p. 102.

The impression given in John's gospel is that Jesus did not see his role as being involved in political affairs. During the events which led up to his death, by the typical Roman method of crucifixion, he apparently advocated non-violence. When his disciple Peter, who was later to be regarded as the founder of the Church and the first pope, drew his sword to defend his master, cutting off the right ear of one of the Jewish High Priest's servants in the process, he was firmly told by Jesus to put the weapon away.

> Put your sword back in its scabbard; am I not to drink the cup that the father has given me?. [John 18:11. This and subsequent quotations are from the *Jerusalem Bible*. See Bibliography.]

Later, when brought before Pilate, he stated that,

> Mine is not a kingdom of this world; if my kingdom were of this world, my men would have fought to prevent my being surrendered to the Jews. But my kingdom is not of this kind. [John 18:36]

Yet such pronouncements still left a problem for Jesus's followers, who were apparently first called 'Christians' in Antioch in the early years of the reign of the Roman emperor Claudius [41-54 A.D., Acts of the Apostles 11:26]. According to Matthew's gospel, Jesus saw himself, despite what he said to Peter in the garden of Gethsemane, as a bringer of conflict as well as peace and reconciliation.

> Do not suppose that I have come to bring peace to the earth: it is not peace I have come to bring but a sword. For I have come to set a man against his father, a daughter against her mother, a daughter-in-law against her mother-in-law. A man's enemies will be those of his own household. [Matthew 10:34-6, v.36 being in large part a quotation from the Jewish prophet Micah's description of the social injustice of his own day, in 7:6.]

All these texts, though, and many others in the New Testament, were concerned with the concept of 'the kingdom of God', which is already to be found in the Jewish psalms [for example 22:28 and 45:6], but is greatly developed in the teachings of Jesus. It is already proclaimed in John the Baptist's message of repentance [Matthew 3:2] and is frequently referred to in chapters 8 to 13 of Matthew's gospel, as well as in Mark and Luke's gospels. The question is, and was to be for medieval Christians, what kind of kingdom was this to be?

'The Two Cities'

In the preaching of the kingdom by Jesus in Matthew 8-13, there is no sign that it has anything to do with political authority. The signs of the coming of this kingdom may have involved defying some of the commandments and practices of the Jewish Law, or **Torah**, as well as help to the poor and the healing of the sick, but they did not apparently require the overthrow of the existing political regime, which at that time in Israel or Palestine[11] involved native rulers under the overall authority of Rome. Indeed, when Jesus was directly confronted by other Jewish leaders with the question of what attitude religious Jews should adopt towards the Roman authorities and their 'native' puppets, he replied with the famous declaration, 'Give back to Cæsar what belongs to Cæsar – and to God what belongs to God' [Matthew 22:21], which, like the statement in John's gospel, strongly implied a separation of powers (or 'swords') between religious and political authorities. The debate about the proper interpretation of these and other texts has gone on ever since, but the important point to note here is that much of the politics of the Middle Ages was to revolve around this particular problem. In addition, the inclusion of the texts in chapter 1 is intended to demonstrate from the outset that much of the treatment of European Jews, in the period up to the Reformation and thereafter, was to be a practical result of the controversies within 'Christendom' on the subject of authority, whether ecclesiastical or secular.

Crucial to this debate was the book which became the last of the 'New Testament' (as it was known to medieval Christians), that is, the 'Apocalypse', or revelation of St John. Almost certainly not written by the gospel-writer and 'beloved disciple' himself, this text nonetheless appears to have emerged from that apostle's circle, towards the end of the first century. It continues a Jewish tradition of writings which purport to describe hidden supernatural events, often to come in the future, by means of highly coloured and metaphorical language. The most notable Jewish example was the book of Daniel, which in modern Bibles is divided between the Old Testament and the 'inter-testamentary' writings known as the 'Apocrypha', and which is often excluded from Protestant Bibles today but was well known in the fifteenth and sixteenth centuries. The significant point for religious and political

11 In the Hebrew Bible, Palestine meant the land of the Philistines. It only came to mean the whole of **Canaan** in the first century of the Christian era. [W. M. Clow, *The Bible reader's encyclopædia and concordance*, London, 1962, p. 272.]

discussion in the medieval and early modern periods was that John took up the Jewish author's attack on Babylon, the symbolic enemy of Israel, and transferred all the enmity and symbolism to the then current enemy, Rome. Thus Rome/Babylon was, for the author of Revelation, the fallen city,

> haunt of devils and a lodging for every foul spirit and dirty, loathsome bird. All the nations have been intoxicated by the wine of her prostitution; every king in the earth has committed fornication with her, and every merchant grown rich through her debauchery [Revelation 18:3].

In contrast, John saw a vision of another, holy city named Jerusalem, which was shortly to descend from heaven to earth, 'as beautiful as a bride all dressed for her husband', where God would live 'among men' [Revelation 21:2-3]. The most significant development of this power-ful image, as far as medieval and early modern theologians were concerned, was that achieved by the North African bishop and theologian, Augustine of Hippo. He converted to Christianity in Milan, in 386, after years of close association with the dualist movement known as Manichæism,[12] which was strong at the time in the land of his birth [in modern Algeria]. He was to be an immensely significant figure in the history of Western Christendom, both before and after the Reformation, not least in the development of the Church's attitudes to Jews.[13] Augustine developed considerably this image of the 'two cities', heavenly and earthly, in his greatest and best-known work, *The City of God*.[14] This intricate and elaborate develop-ment of the concept included in John's Revelation was to be highly influential in the centuries up to 1400, and long after. The notion of an opposition between the heavenly and the earthly cities was faithfully reproduced, for example, by the twelfth century German writer, Otto of Freising and many others.[15] However, Augustine also had some significant things to say about Jews.

It was inevitable that a Christian vision of the heavenly city, transferred to earth, on the lines of the 'great commission' given by Jesus to his

12 A group of people, associated with the third-century Iranian Manes, or Manichæus, who believed that there were two equal Gods, God the Father and Satan, who represented, respectively, the forces of good and evil in the world.

13 A fine biography is that of P. R. L. Brown, *Augustine of Hippo*, London, 1967.

14 Saint Augustine, *The City of God*, trans. John Healey, ed. R. V. G. Tasker, 2 vols, London, 1945.

15 Otto of Freising, *The two cities. A chronicle of universal history to the year 1146 A.D.*, trans. C. C. Mierow, New York, 1966.

disciples, according to the last two verses of Matthew's gospel ['Go therefore, make disciples of all the nations; baptise them in the name of the Father, and of the Son and of the Holy Spirit, and teach them to observe all the commands I gave you.' Matthew 28:19-20], would have to face up to the 'problem' of the continued existence of Jews who rejected Christian claims. Augustine did not refuse the challenge.

Augustine and the Jews

Two chapters of the *City of God* specifically address this question. In the first [bk. 18 ch. 46], Augustine has no doubt that the Jewish people was responsible for its own fate at the hands of the Romans.

> But the Jews who rejected Him, and slew Him (according to the needfulness of His death and resurrection), after that were miserably spoiled by the Romans, under the domination of strangers, and dispersed over the face of the whole earth.

However, following Paul [Romans 11:11, see document 1], he did not consign all subsequent Jews to destruction as a consequence, indeed he saw the Jewish diaspora, or dispersion, as part of God's will, for their good and that of Christians. Augustine first quotes from Psalm 59, using one Latin version, although another absolutely contradicts this meaning [a warning for translators and for their readers, see the Note on the Documents, p. xiv].

> God will let me see my desires upon my enemies. Slay them not, lest my people forget it, but scatter them abroad with my power.[16]

Whatever the original meaning of the psalm may have been, Augustine's version led him to 'allow' Jews a role in God's plan for the world's salvation, and hence security from violence or even extermination. Referring to Psalm 59, he writes:

> Here did God show mercy to His Church, even by means of the Jews His enemies, because, as the Apostle [Paul] says, 'through their fall cometh salvation to the Gentiles'. And therefore he slew them not, that is, he left them their name of Jews still, although they be the Romans' slaves, lest

16 The alternative Latin text was approved for liturgical use by Pope Pius XII on 24 March 1945 [*Biblia sacra iuxta vulgatam clementinam*, ed. Alberto Colunga, O.P. and Laurentio Turrado, Madrid, 1977, p. 449n]. The *Jerusalem Bible* thus has: 'Slaughter them, God before my people forget! Harry them with your power and strike them down, Lord, our shield!' [p. 726].

their utter dissolution should make us forget the law of God concerning this testimony of theirs. So it were nothing to say, 'Slay them not', but that he adds 'Scatter them abroad': For if they were not dispersed throughout the whole world with their scriptures, the Church would lack their testimonies concerning those prophecies fulfilled in our Messiah.[17]

The immense prestige of Augustine and his writings ensured that, at least up to the twelfth century, there was no direct pressure for the elimination of Jews from Christian society, or for active efforts to be made to convert them. Again, the *City of God* indicated the policy which was to be adopted. In chapter 29 of book 20, Augustine commented on a text from the Jewish prophet Malachi:

Know that I am going to send you Elijah the prophet before my day comes, that great and terrible day. He shall turn the hearts of fathers towards their children and the hearts of children towards their fathers, lest I come and strike the land with a curse. [Malachi 3:23-4 in the *Jerusalem Bible*, 4:5-6 in other versions.]

The bishop of Hippo interpreted Malachi's words in a manner most positive for the Jews of his own day and, as it turned out, for those of the later medieval and early modern periods. After discussing various earlier commentaries on this text, Augustine writes:

There may be a farther and more choice interpretation of this place [text], namely, that Elijah should turn the heart of the Father unto the Child [understood here to mean Jesus]; not by making the Father to love the Child, but by teaching that the Father loves Him, that the Jews who had hated Him before may henceforth love him also.

It was clearly not Augustine's intention that Judaism should continue for ever as a separate religion, but rather that the 'remnant' should come to the truth in the fullness of time. This, indeed, was the true meaning of Elijah's predicted reappearance, in the Christian and Jewish prophetic traditions. For Jews, he was the precursor of the **Messiah**, who is still to come in the future, while for the Christian gospel writers he was identified with John the Baptist [Matthew 11:14: 'And he, if you will believe me, is the Elijah who was to return.']. Messianic movements among Jews, Christians and converted Jews in Spain were to be a phenomenon of the period of the 1492 expulsion of the Jews from Spain [see introduction to chapter II and documents 14 and 15].

17 Augustine, *City of God*, p. 221.

The Church and the Jews, c. 1050-1215

In the meantime, though, the Western Church, under the leadership of a Papacy which was increasingly flexing its muscles in the period after 1050,[18] felt the need to formulate a 'policy' towards those Jews who were living among the Catholic faithful. Up until about 1200, it seems clear that Augustine's views prevailed, both in the works of commentators and polemicists, and in the pronouncements of popes and Church councils. As far as the late medieval Church was concerned, the basis for the treatment of Jews, by both ecclesiastical and secular authorities, was to be found in the decrees of the Fourth Lateran Council of the Roman Church, which were issued in 1215 [see introduction to chapter I]. These pronouncements were intended not only to rule the Church's own affairs but also to be incorporated into the legislation of Catholic states, for example in Spain [see document 4 (i) and (ii) for the case of Castile]. Historically, the Church had tended, even in countries, including Italy and even Rome itself, to obtain its knowledge and form its opinion of Judaism not from the experience of living Jews but rather from the pages of Scripture and from later Christian commentaries upon it. As a result, a partial consensus had emerged amongst clerics and laypeople, whether educated or uneducated.

The outlines of this consensus were as follows. It was generally agreed that, eventually, all Jews would convert to Christianity and Judaism as such would cease to exist. Augustine's views were faithfully reproduced by eleventh- and twelfth-century commentators, such as the disciples of Anselm of Canterbury (c. 1033-1109), and others influenced by him, who included Odo of Cambrai, William of Champeaux, and even the controversial Peter Abelard. These writers, while admitting the need for the Jewish 'remnant' to be preserved within Christian society, without violence or persecution being undertaken against it, nonetheless continued the old habit of drawing their evidence of Judaism from the Bible, rather than their actual Jewish neighbours.[19] However, as will soon become apparent, changes in the Church's approach to Jews and Judaism were to appear thereafter,

18 For the growing strength of the Papacy in the period from 1050 to 1250, see, for example, Walter Ullmann, *A short history of the Papacy*, London, 1972; B. Tierney, *The crisis of Church and state, 1050-1300*, Englewood Cliffs, N.J., 1964; Colin Morris, *The Papal monarchy: the Western Church, 1050-1250*, Oxford, 1988.

19 These writers are more fully discussed in Jeremy Cohen, *The friars and the Jews. The evolution of medieval anti-Judaism*, Ithaca and London, 1982, pp. 25-6 and notes.

which affect the actions of secular governments as well. In the meantime, though, it is necessary to place this theological debate in its historical context, and, in order to do this, a discussion and assessment is required of the sources which are to be presented below.

The Documents[20]

It is quite proper that this Introduction should have started with a discussion, both of the origins and development of Jewish settlement and life in medieval Western and Central Europe, and of the response of the Christian, or Catholic, Church to the Jewish presence, as these will be the main themes of all that follows. A wide variety of different kinds of text is presented here, and their strengths and weaknesses are shortly to be considered. However, one limitation has to be noted at the start. This is that the necessary restriction to written texts inevitably excludes many other ways in which both Jews and Christians experienced religion in the fifteenth and sixteenth centuries. In recent years, much work has been done on this subject, particularly in relation to Christianity, and the result is that scholars are increasingly appreciating the importance of auditory, visual and other sensual inputs in the experiencing and living of religious teaching and practice. This point is rightly stressed, elsewhere in this series, by Robert Swanson, who writes, when discussing the written sources for English religious life (all Christian, of course) in the late Middle Ages:

> But some elements are irrecoverable, or very imperfectly recoverable: the emotional responses which were generated by participation in this continuity of celebrations, from presence at plays to attendance at services and processions, and being caught up in the drama and emotional appeal of the liturgy, to responses to the increasingly complex polyphonic music of the age.[21]

Not only was all this true for Christians in other European countries as well but Jews, too, despite strict religious controls on the use of

---

20 See also the Note on the Documents above, p. xii–xvi.

21 Swanson, *Catholic England*, pp. 5-6 and 'Medieval liturgy as theatre: the props', *Studies in Church History*, XXIX, 1992, pp. 239-53. For England, see also Duffy, *Stripping of the altars*. A good Continental study which also addresses the question of the variety of religious experience is William A. Christian, Jr, *Local religion in sixteenth-century Spain*, Princeton, 1981.

images,[22] produced pictorial art, in the form of manuscript illuminations, which portrayed religious as well as secular life. Such examples survive from the late medieval period in Spain, France, Italy and Germany.[23]

Nevertheless, it is clear that written sources, most of them translated here for the first time, can illuminate many aspects of the role and experience of European Jews in this period. Dividing the selection into chapters has, however, been somewhat difficult, as, in the late medieval and early modern periods (and indeed in many others!), it is impossible to make a precise distinction between religious matters and political, social and economic questions. This point is fundamental to the self-understanding, and hence to the modern reader's comprehension, of Jews and Christians in this period. Thus it seems proper that the documentary selection should begin with extracts from the Bible.[24] As the theme of the first chapter is 'The Church and the Jews', these texts are presented in preference to the shared books of the Hebrew Bible. The purpose is to present a Christian viewpoint, which will, it is hoped, be counteracted by other documents in this selection. The Biblical texts were, however, the basic vocabulary of relations, of whatever kind, between Christians and Jews in this period and only one further point needs to be made about them at this stage. It should always be remembered that both Jews and Christians in the fifteenth and sixteenth centuries believed the texts of the Bible to be the inspired Word of God, and indeed of Divine authorship, though produced by human hands. Adherents of the two religions might differ widely in their manner of interpreting Biblical texts (and Jews did not regard the Christian New Testament as Biblical at all), but this basic viewpoint must be borne in mind by the modern reader. During the period covered by this work, Christian scholars were beginning to be aware of the importance of textual accuracy, and of the limitations of the Latin 'Vulgate' translation from Hebrew and Greek which was then in use in the Western Church [see the Note on the Documents above, p. xiv], but they did not engage in the kind of debate about the dating and authorship of the books of the Bible which concerns so many modern scholars. Having made that point it is time to move on to

---

22 'You shall not make yourself a carved image or any likeness of anything in heaven or on earth beneath or in the waters under the earth; you shall not bow down to them or serve them. For I, Yahweh your God, am a jealous God.' [Exodus 20:4-5. See also Deuteronomy 5:8-9.]

23 Thérèse and Mendel Metzger, *Jewish Life in the Middle Ages. Illuminated Hebrew manuscripts of the thirteenth to sixteenth centuries*, New York, 1982.

24 Document 1 and introduction to chapter 1.

consider the other types of text which are represented in this selection, and which may properly be included under the heading 'religious'.

Documents issued by the Curia, or Court, of the Roman Popes are a major source for Christian-Jewish relations in this period, and are well represented here.[25] Since the mid-twelfth century at least, the Curia had been a centre of power (and, in the view of many, corruption) for much of the Western Church. The Popes claimed to control all the Church's affairs, but the main business of the Curia was in ecclesiastical jobs and legal cases concerning both clerics and laypeople.[26] The question of the Jews came within the remit of the Popes for two reasons. Firstly, as heads of Western Christendom, they had to have a policy on this subject and were responsible for interpreting the Scriptures to the Catholic faithful in this and other matters, and secondly, they had Jewish subjects of their own in the normal, secular sense, in southeastern France, including Avignon, Vienne and Carpentras, and in a band across the centre of Italy, including Rome itself. Thus the papal documents in this collection concern not only directly theological and spiritual matters but also the economic, social, religious and cultural activities of Jews, as individuals and as communities. The general question of the authorship of this category of source has been considered in the Note on the Documents, but it is worth noting at this stage that all may have had a specifically papal hand in them, and in particular those which were concerned with theological matters. In general terms, the administrative documents are concerned with individual cases and are as likely to be objective as any of the secular legislation which is considered below, while the specifically religious texts may have to be judged by different standards, which will also be discussed in due course.

The Inquisitorial sources in this collection are of two types. Firstly, there are inquisitorial manuals.[27] The Inquisition, a term which originally meant any kind of official inquiry, was, in this particular case, a specialised tribunal set up in the 1230s by Pope Gregory IX to discover 'unorthodox' views among Christians, especially in the south of France and northern Italy.[28] In the first two decades of its operation,

25 Documents 2, 7, 9, 21, 29 (ii), 30, 35 (iii), 38, 44, 45, 47.

26 See note 18, above.

27 Documents 3 and 4 (iii).

28 The best brief introduction to the Papal Inquisition and its early work is Bernard Hamilton, *The Medieval Inquisition*, London, 1981. Also see W. A. Wakefield, *Heresy, Crusade and Inquisition in southern France, 1100-1250*, London, 1974.

there was no mandatory control over the inquisitors' actions, and the powers originally granted by the Papacy enabled often young and inexperienced friars to arrest people summarily and even burn them for heresy without any kind of legal process. Inevitably, and properly, as it may seem, the ecclesiastical lawyers went to work to try to ensure that such excesses would not occur in the future. It may, however, be asked how Jews came to be involved with the Inquisition, as the extracts from the manuals and from Inquisition trials[29] clearly indicate that they were. The answer to this question is to be found in documents 3 (i) and (ii) and 4 (iii),[30] but at this stage it is necessary only to note firstly, that inquisitors' manuals, such as those quoted here, were intended by their authors to guide colleagues both in procedure and in the identification of heretical or unorthodox beliefs. The *Dictionary of the Inquisitors*, a Spanish source published in 1494, is a late and refined version of the form which had been developed in the fourteenth century by, for example, the Frenchman Bernard Gui and the Catalan Nicolau Eymerich. The most obvious defect of these earlier manuals is their tendency to categorise heretical Christian ideas of their own day in terms of the heresies of the early Church. In the case of Judaism, this approach not surprisingly led to the continuance, into the early modern period, of a disregard for the living experience of European Jews, in favour of stereotyped ideas drawn from a traditional interpretation of Biblical texts. The case of Inquisition trials, however, is somewhat different.

Both the Papal and the separate Spanish Inquisitions of the fifteenth and sixteenth centuries had as their primary purpose the reconciliation of heretics to the Church, so that the former offenders might be fully restored to its life. In both cases, extensive records of the resulting trials survive in the archives of Spain and Italy. The texts presented here involve the ambiguities of existence for Jewish 'converts' to Christianity who were believed to have reverted to the beliefs and practices of their former religion.[31] In four cases, the identification of such 'judaisers', as they were known in the Inquisition's extensive jargon, was made by means of ritual practices associated with the law of Moses, while in the fifth [Document 39], the issue was a supposed case of the abuse and ritual murder of a Christian child in Spain in 1490. The wider issues involved in these trials will be considered

29 Documents 3, 4.
30 See also the introduction to chapter I.
31 Documents 5, 6, 11, 17, 39.

below, but at this stage it is necessary to consider the value, if any, of such evidence to the historian of Jews and Christians, including converts, in the Europe of the period. This is a highly controversial subject. Some scholars, not all of them Jewish, have asserted that the bias and avowed purpose of Inquisitorial tribunals invalidate all the material they collected as evidence of anyone's religious belief and practice.[32] Others, however, while recognising the obvious pitfalls, nevertheless take the view that it is indeed possible to obtain considerable, and in some cases unique, evidence from Inquisitorial records. As Brian Pullan has written, these trial documents at the very least have the potential to be 'the key which unlocks the mind of the people, rather than merely revealing their public acts and their private transactions'.[33] In particular, they provide a rare opportunity to learn about the religious lives of 'ordinary' women of the period, in contrast to the 'great' religious women on whom so much recent literature, including that written from a feminist perspective, has concentrated.[34] Studies of Inquisition trial (and pre-trial) documents, especially in Spain, have provided important information on this subject [see Document 5 (ii)] even though these records, like all the other documents in this book were written by men.[35] This a significant point, which ought not to be forgotten.

In a sense, the other kinds of sources used in this collection which may generally be termed 'religious' are rather more straightforward, although

32 See, for example, Ellis Rivkin, 'The utilisation of non-Jewish sources for the reconstruction of Jewish history', *Jewish Quarterly Review, XLVII*, 1957-8, p. 193, and 'How Jewish were the New Christians?', in Josep M. Solà, Samuel G. Armistead and Joseph H. Silverman, eds, *Hispania Judaica: Studies on the History, Language and Literature of the Jews in the Hispanic World*, I. *History*, Barcelona, 1980, pp. 105-15; C. John Sommerville, 'Debate. Religious faith, doubt and atheism. Comment', *Past and Present*, 128, 1990, p. 154.

33 Brian Pullan, *The Jews of Europe and the Inquisition of Venice, 1550-1670*, Oxford, 1983, p. 117. For further debate on this subject, see Edwards, 'Religious faith and doubt in late medieval Spain: Soria *circa* 1450-1500', *Past and Present*, 120, 1988, pp. 4-5 and 'Why the Spanish Inquisition?', *Studies in Church History*, XXIX, 1992, pp. 227-9.

34 For example, Eleanor McLaughlin, 'Women, power and the pursuit of holiness in medieval Christianity', in *Feminist theology. A reader*, ed. Ann Loades, London, 1990, pp. 99-123; Benedicta Ward, 'Saints and sibyls: Hildegard of Bingen to Teresa of Avila', in *After Eve. Women, theology and the Christian tradition*, ed. Janet Martin Soskice, London, 1990, pp. 103-18.

35 Renée C. Levine [Melamed], 'Women in Spanish crypto-Judaism, 1492-1520', unpublished Ph.D. thesis, Brandeis, 1982; Edwards, 'Male and female religious experience among Spanish "New Christians", 1450-1500', in *The expulsion of the Jews: 1492 and after*, ed. Raymond B. Waddington and Arthur Williamson, New York and London, 1994, pp. 41-51.

their relevant features still need to be outlined. In chapter V, extracts from the writings of two of the most important Reformers of the Western Church, Martin Luther and Jean Calvin, as well as those of the distinguished scholar and theologian Desiderius Erasmus, are included.[36] As they concern very much the same matters as the Papal pronouncements on the theological, and the social, position of the Jews, they should be regarded as being very much in the same category as the Roman Catholic documents of that kind. The impact, if any, of the Reformation on the life of Europe's Jews will be considered below, but in terms of the value and nature of sources, the two other kinds of Jewish text which are presented here, and which may properly be classified as 'religious', are of greater interest. Marc Saperstein's anthology of late medieval and early modern Jewish preaching,[37] extracts from which are offered here, draws attention to a vital source for the understanding of Jewish life in Europe in the period. The recording of Jewish sermons was as haphazard as that of their Christian equivalents, yet, as the editor of the anthology remarks, the comments included in them are often closer in time to the events to which they refer than are the chronicles which recorded them for posterity. In a sense it might be more appropriate to include them among the literary than the religious sources in terms of the categories that are being employed here, because they commonly survive as a part of other published work. As with so much recorded Jewish preaching of this period, the selection included here shows a certain bias towards southern Europe. Isaac Arama is regarded as one of the most influential Jewish preachers in the period of the Spanish expulsion,[38] while Joseph ibn Shem Tob directly addresses the difficulties experienced by Jews in Spain in his own period (see introduction to chapter II below).[39] Judah Moscato, on the other hand, in a sermon preached in Mantua in about 1585, indicates that educated Italian Jews were fully immersed in the scholarly, as well as the social, life of the general population in the Renaissance period.[40]

The other Jewish religious source which is used here, in relation to the issue (increasingly important as the sixteenth century progressed) of how converts from Judaism to Christianity should be treated [document

---

36 Documents 40 (i) and (ii), 41 and 42.

37 Marc Saperstein, *Jewish preaching, 1200–1800. An anthology*, New Haven and London, 1989.

38 Document 43 (i).

39 Document 43 (ii).

40 Document 43 (iii).

20], is that of rabbinical 'responses'. As Saperstein points out, these legal rulings, given by Jewish **rabbis** in response to requests, generally from individuals, for interpretation of Biblical and rabbinical Law (**Torah** and **Talmud**) in specific cases, were more likely to be preserved than other kinds of Jewish written output from the period.[41] In various respects they are equivalent to the legal documents issued for Christians by the Papacy, which have already been referred to. As in the Catholic Church, decisions by legal scholars in individual cases might well be generalised in application. There is no great complication in their use by the historian although the same could not be said of the textual work and reasoning which lay behind them.

A considerable range of material concerned with social and economic relations between Jews and Christians is included in this selection, and it takes various forms. Much is secular legislation or edicts, issued by rulers of various states, such as monarchies, especially in Spain, and Italian states such as the duchy of Milan and the territories of the Popes themselves (see above, p. 16).[42] Once again, some of these texts were intended to be applied generally within the territories concerned, while others dealt with specific cases. Some examples of private contracts and litigation involving Jews and Christians are included, as well as an interesting piece of communal legislation from Spain, the laws of Valladolid of 1432.[43]

Finally, it is necessary to look at a third category of source which may be broadly referred to as 'literary'. Once again, it is hard to distinguish precisely between one category and another, given that the examples given here of chronicles,[44] personal correspondence,[45] poetry,[46] autobiography[47] and even a novel,[48] share the characteristic that, while they

---

41 Saperstein, *Jewish preaching*, p. 5.

42 Documents 4 (i) and (ii), 8, 10, 11, 13, 22, 24 (i), 25, 26, 27, 31 (i), 32, 33, 35, 36, 37 (i). For the nature of the authority of Christian rulers over Jews in medieval and early modern Europe, see Gavin I. Langmuir's discussion of the French case in '*Judei nostri* and the beginning of Capetian legislation' and '*Tanquam servi*: The change in Jewish status in French law about 1200', in *Toward a definition of Antisemitism*, Berkeley, Los Angeles, Oxford, 1990, pp. 137-66 and 167-94.

43 Documents 29 (i), 34, 45; excerpts from the 1432 laws are in documents 24 (ii) and 31 (ii).

44 Documents 12, 16, 18, 23, 39 (vi).

45 Documents 40 (ii), (iii) and (v).

46 Document 19.

47 Document 49.

48 Document 48.

are all in their different ways intensely personal, they constantly reflect on the same issues as arise in the more 'public' sources which are included here.

'Religion'

One point which emerges clearly from all these texts is the predominance of religion, whether as Judaism or Christianity, in the life of these Europeans of the fifteenth and sixteenth centuries. Something must therefore be said about what it means when the word 'religion' is used in historical material, whether primary, as in the case of this selection of documents, or secondary, as in that of the commentary upon them which is provided here. In recent years, this matter has begun once again to excite the attention of scholars, as attempts are made to reconcile the former extremes which have dominated the subject for so many decades. So often, religion has been seen either as a matter of purely individual experience, as it was by William James, brother of the novelist Henry,[49] or as the result of impersonal social and economic forces, as in the Marxist tradition. Now, however, the discussion seems to take a rather different form. Some years ago, it was suggested that 'religious' phenomena might be subdivided in terms of the old debate, into the individual and private on the one hand and the communal and public on the other. However, a third category was included in the discussion, that is, the intellectual constructs concerned with God which are commonly known as theology, or doctrine.[50] There is no doubt that many or most of the documents presented here testify, in their various ways, to the importance of this third category. The value of doctrine and theology as guides to any real human experience has, however, been subjected to assault by Gavin Langmuir, who has attempted to raise the profile and status of individual 'religious' experience by coining a new use for the word 'religiosity'. In common parlance, this is not a particularly complimentary word with which to describe 'religious' people. In current English dictionaries,[51] the expression hovers uneasily between the polite

---

49 William James, *The varieties of religious experience*, Cambridge, Mass., 1985. A full discussion of the merits and demerits of this work is to be found in Nicholas Lash, *Easter in ordinary. Reflections on human experience and the knowledge of God*, London, 1988.

50 Edwards, 'The *conversos*: a theological approach', *Bulletin of Hispanic Studies*, LXII, 1985, 39-49.

51 For example, *The concise Oxford dictionary*, eighth edition, 1992.

'religious' and the less polite 'religiose', defined as 'excessively religious'. For Langmuir, 'religion' corresponds to 'official' religious
teaching and doctrine, as represented here by the words of Popes,
rabbis and theologians, while 'religiosity' describes the religious life of
individuals, including Jews who found themselves in trouble with
Christian authorities, or converts from Judaism to Christianity who
were investigated or tried by the Inquisition.[52] Here, the general
assumption has been made that, as Leszek Kolakowski put it, 'what
people mean in religious discourse is what they ostensibly mean'.[53]
Thus, for the purpose of what follows, it has not been regarded as
necessary to make guesses concerning the real motives of the
individuals and groups who appear or are referred to in these
documents. The pitfalls of language have already been alluded to (see
the Note on the Documents), but to understand these events and
people's actions, it is essential that we realise the extent to which most
people saw everything in religious terms. This is not of course to say
that, in Langmuir's terms, the 'religiosity' of individuals was necessarily identical to the 'religion' of public bodies and institutions. Doubt
about the fundamentals of life and the faith were as much a feature of
the late medieval and early modern periods as they are of the present
day.[54] Indeed, such doubts were to be a particular problem for converts
from Judaism in Spain who, having left one strong tradition, Judaism,
often found it hard to adopt another, Christianity.[55]

A Jewish life?

The general conditions of life of Europe's Jews are normally assumed
to have declined in the period under consideration here. There does
indeed seem to be some truth in Cohen's assertion that the 'discovery'
of rabbinical Judaism, in the form of the Talmud, in the thirteenth
century seriously threatened Jewish life by allowing the new Christian
religious orders of friars, particularly Franciscan and Dominican, to
make Jews a target as part of their campaign against heresy and in

52 Gavin I. Langmuir, *History, religion and Antisemitism*, Berkeley, Los Angeles and
   Oxford, 1990, pp. 133–200.

53 Leszek Kolakowski, *Religion: if there is no God*, Glasgow, 1982, p. 16.

54 Edwards, 'Religious faith and doubt', p. 3 and 'Debate. Religious faith, doubt and
   atheism', pp. 158–60; Langmuir, 'Doubt in Christendom', in *Toward a definition of
   Anti-semitism*, Berkeley, Los Angeles and Oxford, 1990, pp. 100–33.

55 Kenneth R. Scholberg, *Satira e invectiva en la España medieval*, Madrid, 1971, pp.
   303–60.

favour of what they perceived to be a truly 'Christian' society.[56] In that sense, the Spanish Inquisition, whose records have provided many of the sources which are used here, simply represented the continuation of the attempt by the Catholic Church and secular authorities to implement a religious and social prescription, which attempted to realise the vision of the fathers of the Fourth Lateran Council of 1215. The difference was that, by the beginning of the fifteenth century, there was a large population, mainly in Castile and Aragon, of 'New Christian' converts from Judaism.[57] As chapter V suggests, the Reformation did little to improve the lot of Europe's Jews, either in the sixteenth century or later.[58] Indeed, as far as the Roman Church is concerned, it seems to have made things worse, at least for those Jews who found themselves under the direct rule of the Papacy. Not only was the attack on the Talmud renewed, but increasingly oppressive measures were taken against Jews in the Papal states.[59]

Nonetheless, it is hoped that no reader of chapter VI of this selection will go away with the impression that Jews lived a constantly wretched life in Western and Central Europe in the period between 1400 and 1600. Despite religious and social restrictions, and false accusations of violent atrocities against Christians which caused oppression of Jewish communities in Spain, Italy and elsewhere,[60] it was possible for Jews (at least male ones) to exercise some power in that society. Western Jewry survived the expulsions and lived to see some revival of its fortunes, with the growth of the Polish community and the restoration and development of those in the Netherlands and England. Whatever the theologians and politicians may have said, Jewish life among Christians was possible during the Renaissance and Reformation and contributed far more to it than Hobsbawm and other 'modernists' seem to have dreamt of.

---

56 Cohen, *The friars and the Jews*, pp. 242-64.

57 Document 5 and Edwards, *The Jews in Christian Europe*, pp. 15-17, 27-30.

58 Introduction to chapter V and Edwards, *The Jews in Christian Europe*, pp. 50-63.

59 Document 7 and Edwards, *The Jews in Christian Europe*, pp. 66-92.

60 See the discussions of the 'ritual murder' accusations in Edwards, 'Why the Spanish Inquisition?' pp. 229-30 and Langmuir, 'Thomas of Monmouth: detector of ritual murder', and 'The knight's tale of young Hugh of Lincoln', in *Toward a definition of Antisemitism*, pp. 209-36 and 237-62.

I: The Church and the Jews

As the very foundation of the medieval Church's attitude to the Jews was Scripture, it is proper to begin with some of the texts which particularly influenced the teaching given to Catholics. Included here are some verses from the Gospels and from one of Paul's epistles. These passages are presented in the Latin of the Vulgate Bible, in which they would have been heard at the time, as well as in a modern English translation.[1] In Catholic liturgies of the late medieval and early modern periods, this extract from Matthew's gospel would have been sung, often in a somewhat dramatised form, on Palm Sunday, when the entry of Jesus to Jerusalem, before his arrest and trial, was commemorated. In it, the Jews appear to take corporate and everlasting responsibility for the Christian Saviour's death. The extract from John's gospel purports to be part of a dialogue between Jesus and Jewish religious leaders, in which Jesus appears to link Jews in general with the devil, an idea which was to gain great popularity and influence in later periods.[2] In contrast, the passage from Paul's epistle to the Romans gives a much more positive view of the relationship between Jews and non-Jewish Christians, though one which has only recently come to prominence in the teaching of the Churches.[3]

In the thirteenth century, the Papacy became aware, through the agency of Christian converts from Judaism, that the elder religion did not rely for inspiration and guidance on the Hebrew Scriptures alone, but also on the rabbinical teachings included in the Talmud.[4] As a result, Pope Gregory IX condemned the Talmud in 1236, on the grounds that it was blasphemous of Christianity and encouraged antisocial behaviour by Jews against Christians.

1 Although some of the vernacular languages spoken in Western and Central Europe in the fifteenth and sixteenth centuries were much closer to the Latin of the Vulgate Bible than was the English of the same period, the argument used by R. N. Swanson, in another work in this series, nonetheless applies in this case: 'The aim of retaining the original languages [in the present volume only one] is to demonstrate the problem of access in a society which was not necessarily Latinate, and the extent to which control of interpretation could be retained by those possessing the linguistic key'. [R. N. Swanson, *Catholic England. Faith, religion and observance before the Reformation*, Manchester University Press, 1993, p. 46.]

2 John Edwards, *The Jews in Christian Europe, 1400-1700*, London, 1991, p. 23; Joshua Trachtenberg, *The Devil and the Jews*, New Haven, 1943.

3 Paul's full treatment of this question is to be found in chapters 9 to 11 of that epistle.

4 See above [Introduction, p. 22] and Edwards, *The Jews*, pp. 20-1.

In this complex, and fairly unreadable, document, the pope accuses these texts, which were a major source for Jewish orthodoxy and life, of encouraging and even instructing Jews to blaspheme against Christianity and to behave in an anti-social manner towards Christians. Formal 'disputations' leading to the condemnation of the Talmud, took place in Paris in 1240 and Barcelona in 1263, and the same arguments were still being deployed by Catholic Christians in the fifteenth and sixteenth centuries, including the earlier insistence that Jews had to be preserved as a remnant of the former Chosen People of God, and not destroyed.⁵

Thereafter, the Papal Inquisition, which had been set up in the reign of that same pope Gregory IX to investigate and repress unorthodox belief within the Church itself, became increasingly interested in Jews, both because of their supposed hostility to the younger faith and because they were suspected of conspiring with Christian heretics against Catholic Christendom. This assault on the religious life and practice of Judaism was carried out under the auspices of the Fourth Lateran Council of the Catholic Church, which, having been called together by Pope Innocent III, had issued its decrees, or canons, in 1215. They were based on the presupposition that:

> *What we strictly forbid, however, is that anyone should dare to break out in insults against the Redeemer. And since we should not shut our eyes to insults which are heaped upon Him who washed away our sins, we decree that such presumptuous persons shall be duly restrained by suitable punishment meted out by the secular rulers, so that none dare blaspheme against Him who was crucified for our sake.⁶*

One of those who attempted to obey this injunction was Alfonso X of Castile (1252-1284). His seven-part law-code, known in Castilian as the Siete Partidas, *included, as chapter 24 of its seventh and last section, a series of laws concerning the kingdom's Jews. The extracts offered here pronounce on the vexed questions of the definition of a 'Jew' and the fate of converts from Judaism to Christianity. Both these matters were to become important issues in the fifteenth and sixteenth centuries.*

By the fourteenth century, inquisitors such as Bernard Gui and Nicolau Eymerich, who compiled handbooks for the guidance of their colleagues,

---

5 See above [Introduction, p. 12] also Edwards, *The Jews*, pp. 19, 29-30. For relevant texts with English translations, see Hyam Maccoby, *Judaism on trial. Jewish-Christian disputations in the Middle Ages*, London and Toronto, 1982.

6 J. D. Mansi, *Sacrorum Conciliorum nova et amplissima collectio*, Florence, 1759-1798, repr. 1962, vol. 22, p. 1055.

thought it necessary to include their own descriptions of Jews and Judaism alongside those of the various heretical movements in Christianity which they saw, or imagined, in their own time. This earlier work was to be taken up in the anonymous Dictionary of the Inquisitors, *published in Spain in 1494, when Ferdinand and Isabella's Spanish Inquisition had been in operation for nearly fifteen years. The 'dictionary entry' translated here reflects the perceived results of the work of local tribunals in Castile and Aragon, which are exemplified by the extract from the trial of a Jewish convert in Trujillo in Spanish Extremadura, in 1489-1490, which is included here, along with a brief extract from a register of statements given to the Soria tribunal in 1501. This is an example of female adherence to Judaism among the converts in Spain. The example of the Spanish Inquisition was imitated, in the next century, by the Venetian inquisitors, who attempted, in their turn, to defend the Christian faith, as they saw it, in a cosmopolitan and multi-religious city.[7] In 1554, Pope Julius III renewed, once again, the thirteenth-century Christian attack on the Talmud. Thus earlier traditions survived both the Reformation and the Counter-Reformation of the Catholic Church.*

1. The New Testament and the Jews

(a) Matthew, chapter 27, vv. 22-26

[from *Biblia sacra iuxta vulgatam clementinam*, ed. Alberto Colunga, O.P., and Laurentio Turrado, Madrid, 1977, p. 990]

[22] Dicit illis Pilatus: Quid igitur faceam de Iesu, qui dicitur Christus? [23] Dicunt omnes: Crucifigatur. Ait illis præses: Quid enim mali fecit? At illi magis clamabant dicentes: Crucifigatur. [24] Videns autem Pilatus quia nihil proficeret, sed magis tumultus fieret: accepta aqua, lavit manos coram populo, dicens: Innocens ego sum a sanguine iusti huius: vos videretis. [25] Et respondens universus populus, dixit: Sanguis eius super nos, et super filios nostros. [26] Tunc dimisit illis Barabbam: Iesum autem flagellatum tradidit eis ut crucifigeretur.

[From *The Jerusalem Bible*, ed. Alexander Jones, London, 1968, p. 42]

[22] 'But in that case', Pilate said to them, 'what am I to do with Jesus who is called Christ?' They all said, 'Let him be crucified'. [23] 'Why?', he asked 'What harm has he done?' But they shouted all the louder, 'Let him be crucified!' [24] Then Pilate saw that he was making no impression, that in fact a riot was imminent. So he took

7 Brian Pullan, *The Jews of Europe and the Inquisition of Venice*, 1550-1670, Oxford, 1983.

some water, washed his hands in front of the crowd and said, 'I am innocent of this man's blood. It is your concern.' [25] And the people, to a man, shouted back, 'His blood be on us and on our children!' [26] Then he released Barabbas for them. He ordered Jesus to be first scourged and then handed over to be crucified.

(b) John, chapter 8, vv. 42-45

[*Biblia vulgata*, p. 1051]

[42] Dixit ergo eis Iesus: Si Deus pater vester esset, diligeretis utique me; ego enim ex Deo processi, et veni; neque enim a me ipso veni, sed ille me misit. [43] Quare loquelam meam non cognoscitis? Quia non potestis audire sermonem meum. [44] Vos ex patre diabolo estis; et desideria patris vestri vultis facere. Ille homicida erat ab initio, et in veritate non stetit; quia non est veritas in eo; cum loquitur mendacium, ex propriis loquitur, quia mendax est, et pater eius. [45] Ego autem si veritatem dico, non creditis mihi.

[*Jerusalem Bible*, p. 130]

[42] Jesus answered: If God were your father, you would love me, since I have come here from God; yes, I have come from him; not that I came because I chose, no, I was sent, and by him. [43] Do you know why you cannot take in what I say? It is because you are unable to understand my language. [44] The devil is your father, and you prefer to do what your father wants. He was a murderer from the start; he was never grounded in the truth; there is no truth in him at all: when he lies he is drawing on his own store, because he is a liar and the father of lies. [45] But as for me, I speak the truth and for that very reason you do not believe me.

(c) Paul's epistle to the Romans, chapter 11, vv. 1-2, 11-24

[*Biblia Vulgata*, p. 1103]

[1] Dico ergo: Numquid Deus repulit populum suum? Absit. Nam et ego israelita sum ex semine Abraham, de tribu Beniamin: [2] non repulit Deus plebem suam, quam præscivit. [11] Dico ergo: Numquid sic offenderunt ut caderent? Absit. Sed illorum delicto, salus est gentibus ut illis æmulentur. [12] Quod si delictum eorum divitiæ mundi, et diminutio eorum divitiæ gentium: quanto magis plenitudo eorum?

[13] Vobis enim dico gentibus. Quamdiu quidem ego sum gentium Apostolus, ministerium meum honorificabo, [14] si quomodo ad æmulandum provocem carnem meam, et salvos faciam aliquos ex illis. [15] Si enim amissio eorum, reconciliatio est mundi: quæ assumptio,

nisi vita ex mortuis? [16] Quod si delibatio sancta est, et massa: et si radix sancta, et rami. [17] Quod si aliqui ex ramis fracti sunt, tu autem cum oleaster estes, insertus es in illis, et socius radicis, et pinguedinis olivæ factus es, [18] noli gloriari adversus ramos. Quod si gloriaris: non tu radicem portas, sed radix te. [19] Dices ergo: Fracti sunt rami ut ego inserar. [20] Bene: propter incredulitatem fracti sunt. Tu autem fide stas; noli altum sapere, sed time. [21] Si enim Deus naturalibus ramis non pepercit: ne forte nec tibi parcat. [22] Vide ergo bonitatem, et severitatem Dei: in eos quidem qui ceciderunt, severitatem: in te autem bonitatem Dei, si permanseris in bonitate, alioquin et tu excideris. [23] Sed et illi, si non permanserint in incredulitate, inserentur: potens est enim Deus iterum inserere illos. [24] Nam si tu ex naturali excisus est oleastro, et contra naturam insertus est in bonam olivam: quanto magis ii qui secundum naturam inserentur suæ naturæ?

[*Jerusalem Bible*, pp. 207-208]

[1] Let me put a further question then: is it possible that God has rejected his people? Of course not. I, an Israelite, descended from Abraham through the tribe of Benjamin, [2] could never agree that God had rejected his people, the people he chose specially long ago. [11] Let me put another question then: have the Jews fallen for ever, or have they just stumbled? Obviously they have not fallen for ever: their fall, though, has saved the pagans in a way the Jews may now well emulate. [12] Think of the extent to which the world, the pagan world, has benefited from their fall and defection - then think how much more it will benefit from the conversion of them all. [13] Let me tell you pagans this: I have been sent to the pagans as their apostle, and I am proud of being sent, [14] but the purpose of it is to make my own people envious of you, and in this way save some of them. [15] Since their rejection meant the reconciliation of the world, do you know what their admission will mean? Nothing less than a resurrection from the dead! [16] A whole batch of bread is made holy if the first handful of dough is made holy. [17] No doubt some of the branches have been cut off, and, like shoots of wild olive, you have been grafted among the rest to share with them the rich sap provided by the olive tree itself, [18] but still, even if you think yourself superior to the other branches, remember that you do not support the root; it is the root that supports you. [19] You will say, 'Those branches were cut off on purpose to let me be grafted in!' True, [20] they were cut off, but through their unbelief; if you still hold firm, it is only thanks

to your faith. Rather than making you proud, that should make you afraid. [21] God did not spare the natural branches, and he is not likely to spare you. [22] Do not forget that God can be severe as well as kind: he is severe to those who fell, and he is kind to you, but only for as long as he chooses to be, otherwise you will find yourself cut off too, [23] and the Jews, if they give up their unbelief, grafted back in your place. God is perfectly able to graft them back again; [24] after all, if you were cut off from your natural wild olive to be grafted unnaturally on to a cultivated olive, it will be much easier for them, the natural branches, to be grafted back on to the tree they came from.

2. Pope Gregory IX's attack on the Talmud

A letter addressed by Pope Gregory in 1236 to the rulers of France, which purports to reveal the blasphemous and anti-Christian nature of the Talmud, the written basis of the rabbinical Judaism of the western European Middle Ages.

[From: Solomon Grayzel, *The Church and the Jews in the thirteenth century*, Philadelphia, 1933; in Latin. The transcribed Hebrew words in this extract are the titles or first words of sections of the Talmud]

(1) The Jews affirm that the **Law** which they call the Talmud was promulgated by God.

It is said, 'The rabbis say, "It happened that a **goy** came before the [famous rabbi] Shammai and said to him, "How many Laws do you have?" Shammai replied, "Two, one written and the other oral"'.

(4) [The Jews] also say that the Law of the Talmud was conserved without being written down until some people appeared whom they call **doctors** and **scribes**, who, out of fear that it might disappear through being forgotten from the memories of men, collected it in a book which considerably exceeds the Bible in length.

(5) In [the Talmudic Law] it is found, among other absurdities, that the said doctors and scribes are superior to the prophets. Rabbi Abdime says, 'Since the day in which the Temple [at Jerusalem] was destroyed [by the Romans in A.D. 70], the gift of prophecy has been taken away from the prophets and given to the doctors [rabbis].

Objection: Is not the rabbi himself a prophet?

[Answer]: Yes, but because this gift has been taken away from the prophets, it has not been given to the rabbis.

[Rabbi] Amemar says: The rabbi is superior to the prophet.

(6) And they say [the rabbis] could overturn the Law [of Moses].

It is said, 'Is it not permitted to overturn the word of the Law?' The Talmud replies and proves that it is. Then it poses several questions and produces several proofs. And in the end it expresses itself thus, 'To sit still and do nothing is something else' [implying to Pope Gregory a willingness to reject Scripture and refuse conversion to Christianity].

(10) Among [the rabbis] are those who have given as a law: 'The best of the Christians, kill him'.

This may be read in *Elle-shemot* [**Exodus**]: 'Pharaoh took six hundred chosen chariots, and all the cavalry of Egypt'. On this, the gloss of Solomon says: Where did these horses come from, for if they belonged to the Egyptians, is it not recounted [in the book of Exodus] that all their beasts were dead? If they belonged to the **Israelites**, did not Moses say: 'All our beasts will leave with us, and not a hoof of theirs will remain' [Exodus 10:26]? Whence, then did these horses come? The answer is that some of Pharaoh's servants, who feared the Word of God, hid their servants and animals. That is why Rabbi Simeon said: The best of the *goyim*, kill him, the best of servants, crush his head'. This means that, since these virtuous and God-fearing Egyptians handed over their animals for the pursuit of the people of God, the best of the Gentiles may be killed like criminals.

(13) And anyone who does not want to have to keep his oath has only to announce at the beginning of the year that the vows and oaths that he may make during the year are null and void.

[Commentary, or gloss] Both [Rabbi Abaye and Rabbi Rabha] agree that the protestation made at the beginning of the year renders null and void all vows made during the year, but Abaye wishes that, at the moment when the vow is made, the protestation should not be remembered, while Rabha says it should.

3. Inquisitors and the Jews

(a) Bernard Gui: France, 1323-4

[From: Bernard Gui, *Le manuel de l'Inquisiteur* (The manual of the Inquisitor), composed in 1323-4, ed. G. Mollat, Paris, 1964, vol. 2, pp. 6-7; in Latin, with French translation]

What follows concerns the perfidy of the Jews against the faith of Christians.

The perfidious Jews struggle, when and where they can, secretly to pervert Christians and draw them into the Jewish perfidy. This is especially the case with those who were formerly Jews and were converted and received **baptism** and the Christian faith, above all those who are closely involved with [the Jews] or are joined to them by links of affinity or else are blood relations.

It has been established, however, that in the case of Christians who may have converted or returned to the Jewish rite, even if they thus returned when they were children or else for fear of death, unless they were absolutely and evidently forced to be baptized, if they confess this [**apostasy**], and whether they are convicted by Christians or Jews, there will be similar proceedings against their supporters, protectors and defenders as [there would be] against the supporters, protectors and defenders of heretics.

(b) Nicolau Eymerich, 1379

[From: Nicolau Eymerich's *Le manuel de l'Inquisiteur*, first published in 1379, with a supplementary comment by Luis Peña, in the Rome, 1578, re-edition, both edited by Luis Sala-Molins, Paris and The Hague, 1977, pp. 72-4; French translation from Latin]

Chapter 17

Christians adhering to Judaism; Jews converting and rejudaising

Must one consider as heretics, and judge as such, those Christians who have converted to Judaism or returned to Judaism, and those who assisted, welcomed or favoured this passage?

Let us subdivide this question so as to consider effectively its three aspects.

Firstly, those Christians who have converted to Judaism, and Jews who, having converted to Christianity, return to the atrocious Jewish **sect** are [indeed] **heretics** and must be considered as such. Both [categories] have renounced the faith of Christ which they had embraced by baptism. If they should wish to abjure the Judaic rite, but do not agree to foreswear Judaism [itself] or do **penance**, they will be pursued like impenitent heretics by bishops and inquisitors, who will hand them over to the **secular arm** to be burnt.

Secondly, those Christians who have favoured or counselled ... a Christian who has gone over to Judaism or returned to Judaism will be considered as aiders and abettors [*fautores*] of heresy and judged as such, for both those who go over to Judaism and those who return to it are heretics.

Thirdly, in the terms of the **bull** *Turbato corde* ['With a disturbed heart'] of our lord pope Nicholas IV, bishops and inquisitors will consider as supporters of heresy those Jews who are favoured in such a manner, whether in the case of the return to Judaism of one of their own, or in that of a Christian adhering to Judaism.

It will be considered that someone has gone over, or returned, to the Judaic rite if he observes its ceremonies, solemnities and **feasts**; if, in short, he does what Jews customarily do.

[To this, Peña adds]

In reality, both Christians converted to Judaism and Jews who have converted and **judaised** again will be treated as apostates. The offence of apostasy and heresy is obvious and hence the inquisitor's intervention is legitimate, whatever the circumstances of the passage or return to Judaism. Even if the Jew who judaises once again received baptism under threat of death or as a child, the offence of 'rejudaisation' remains intact. Nevertheless, a child who falls back into Judaism will be treated with less rigour.

Jews guilty of having contributed in any way to [such] a transfer to Judaism will be condemned to the following penalties: a ban on being in the company of Christians, a fine, imprisonment and a beating. But a particularly severe penalty will fall on a more serious offence, possibly going as far as the surrender of the guilty party to the secular arm [death by burning]. It is for the judge to decide as he sees fit. On this point, such is the common opinion of inquisitors.

It should further be indicated that, in accordance with the provision of Philip II [*Laws of Castile*, Part 1.book 2. chapter 8: Jews and Moors], a Jew who converts to Christianity must change his name. Let him be strongly advised to take one from the Christian **martyrology**, otherwise he will always raise suspicions among others concerning his origins.

4. The 'Jew' defined

(a) A definition of a Jew from the thirteenth-century law-code of Alfonso X of Castile, known as the *Siete Partidas* [*Seven Parts*].

[From: Dwayne E. Carpenter, *Alfonso X and the Jews: an edition of and commentary on 'Siete Partidas'* 7: 24, '*De los judíos*', Modern Philology, 115, Berkeley, Los Angeles, London, 1986, p. 28, in Spanish]

Title 7 Section 24 Law 1.

What the word 'Jew' means and how it acquired this name, and the reasons why the Church and the great Christian lords let them live among them.

Someone is called a Jew who believes in and adheres to the law of Moses as it is stated literally, and is **circumcised** and does the other things that Law of theirs commands. And he took this name from the tribe of **Judah**, which was more noble and more brave than all the other tribes. And, in addition, it had another advantage, that is that the king of the Jews had to be elected from that tribe. And, in addition, during battles, the people from that tribe were always the first to be wounded. And the reason why the Church and the emperors and the kings and other princes suffered the Jews to live among the Christians is this: that they might live in captivity for ever and that they should be a reminder to everyone that they come from the lineage of those who crucified Our Lord Jesus Christ.

(b) A thirteenth-century statement of the Church's view of the conversion of the Jews.

[From Carpenter, *Alfonso X and the Jews*, pp. 33-4; in Spanish]

Law 6. How Jews should not be compelled to become Christians, and what a Jew may gain if he does become a Christian, and what punishment the other Jews deserve who do them harm or dishonour for this reason.

Neither force nor compulsion should be used in any way against any Jew, to make him become a Christian. Rather, the Christians should convert them to faith in Our Lord Jesus Christ by setting a good example, with the sayings of the Holy Scriptures, and with blandishments, for our lord God does not desire or love service which is done to Him under compulsion. Also, we state that if any Jew or Jewess wishes to become a Christian man or woman by his or her own wish, the other Jews should not forbid or prevent them in any way. And if some of [those Jews] stone them or wound or kill them because they wish to become Christians, or after they have been baptised, and if this can be proved, we order that all the murderers and the conspirators in such a murder or stoning should be burnt. And if it should happen that they do not kill, but only wound or dishonour such a person, we order that the judges in the place where this happens should pursue those who do the wounding or inflict the dishonour in order to force them to make amends for their deed. In addition, they should give them such punishment as they think they deserve to receive, for the offence they have committed. Also, we command that, after certain Jews become Christians, all those who live under our lordship should honour them, and no-one should dare to remind them or their families of their Jewish origin in an insulting manner. And that they should possess their property, sharing it with their brothers and inheriting it from their parents, just as if they were [still] Jews. And that they may have all the offices and honours that other Christians have.

(c) A late fifteenth-century Spanish 'definition' which was included in a handbook, or dictionary for inquisitors, published in Valencia in 1494, reflects both the changes and the continuity of attitude in Spain between the compilation of Alfonso X of Castile's *Siete Partidas* in the 1260s and the reign of Ferdinand and Isabella.

[From *Le dictionnaire des inquisiteurs* [1494], ed. L. Sala-Molins, Paris and The Hague, 1981, pp. 269-76; in Latin, with French translation]

The Jews of today remain prisoners of their perfidy and their obstinacy for five reasons.

They say that the Law of Moses was promulgated for its own sake and with another end [than the Christian one] in view. They think this Law must last for ever. [Also] they affirm that the land of Canaan and the city of Jerusalem, with all that they contain, were promised and given to them as a specific prize for their observance of the Law. They believe [also] that the Messiah promised in the Law will free them from their earthly captivity and lead them back to the land of Canaan. As a consequence, they deny that Christ is the true Messiah, and they await another one, who will liberate them. They think, finally, that the Law of the Gospel is imperfect, quite contrary to the Law of Moses, and, as a consequence, sacrilegious and false.

[Here are] three essential reasons for the Jews' refusal to convert, and for their hostility towards the faith of Christ. To start with, they fear poverty. Traditionally greedy, their Law promises them, on numerous occasions, an abundance of material goods: they fear losing them if they convert.

Further, they are brought up from the cradle in the hatred of Christ, of Christianity and of Christians. The Christian Law is totally and constantly cursed in their **synagogues**. Now, that to which men are accustomed from their most tender infancy forms part of their nature ... As a consequence, they abhor those truths which they hold to be errors.

In the third place, they are incapable of converting because of the complexity and sublime nature of what Catholicism suggests they should accept: the divine **Trinity** the double nature and [yet] the oneness of the person of Christ, the sacrament of the **Eucharist**. They are absolutely incapable of understanding, of taking in, these truths, and they think that we adore three gods and that the Eucharist is the worst of idolatries.

They **blasphemed** [Christ's divinity] because they accused him of doing miracles in the name of **Beelzebub**. They put him to death. They persecuted his disciples.

Yet the Church tolerates the Jews as a witness to the Christian faith. She has the duty to sustain and tolerate them in the measure that is possible without outrage to the Creator.

The prince [any ruler] has the right to baptize by force the children of the Jews, always on condition that, as it appears, he does not wish by this means to force adult Jews to receive baptism. By baptism, the young Jew frees himself from his father's power. An adult Jew is not admitted to baptism until he has returned usurious loans.

Converted Jews do not have the right to associate with infidels. Catholics can talk to Jews but they are forbidden to eat in their company.

A Jew cannot have Christian slaves: this would be to sully the Christian religion. But a Christian may buy a Jew.

A Jew or **pagan** who contracts marriage with a blood relation may preserve this bond after conversion.

Jews must not be forced to become Christians. However, the question remains concerning which there has been lengthy discussion: can an inquisitor prosecute Jews? And, if so, on what pretexts? It has been very firmly stated that inquisitors must not concern themselves with Jews because the latter are not within their jurisdiction. It has been said with equal rigour that Jews must not be forcibly baptized and that they must only be brought to renounce their customs by kindness and good words. The **canons** [of Church law] stipulate that only free will can bring a man to conversion. All this is laid down. Nevertheless, either a Jew is guilty of despising our faith and resisting the proper functioning of the Holy Office, or else he is guilty with regard to the Law of Moses, or else he is [guilty] in another matter.

[The writer then gives three examples to illustrate his views on what an inquisitor may or may not do.]

First case. The Jew is guilty with regard to our Law because he fights against it, despises it, or else commits some outrageous act against the Creator or the Redeemer. For example, he profanes churches, altars or sacred ornaments. He obstructs the work of the Inquisition. In this case, the inquisitor can pursue him without the shadow of a doubt, since the defence of the Christian faith has been entrusted to him. It is not at all surprising that, in this case, the Jew falls under the jurisdiction of the inquisitor, since he is guilty of offences under ecclesiastical law....

Second case. The Jews contravene their own Law by practising loans at interest, or by neglecting to observe the commandments of the Jewish Law. The Church does not involve itself [in such cases] unless what [the Jews] do which is contrary to their own Law brings some harm to Christians. Such is the case when they practise usury to the detriment of Christians. It must be said that the inquisitor does not have to intervene in such a case, since this practice [of usury], chosen as an example, does not come within his proper jurisdiction, which extends over all that concerns the Faith, and that alone. But the [local] bishop, as judge in ordinary, can punish [such] Jews under the title of his ordinary jurisdiction. The offence of usury is an offence that concerns both Laws [Jewish and Christian]. Jewish usurers can, as a consequence, be given punishment in their persons by the Church. But [it may be objected], if they may be punished in their persons by the Church, why does the Pope order the secular powers to constrain them? In reality, the papal order is directed to the secular powers in places where the Church itself holds temporal jurisdiction. Where she does not hold [this jurisdiction], she punishes directly, as has just been seen, always seeking the aid of the secular arm. This is because of the mixed character of the offence [i.e. against both ecclesiastical and secular law].

[This applies to] also, those Jews who sin against nature [at that time in Spain, this normally meant homosexuality]. God punishes both Jews and infidels who commit this sin. What God does, his vicar [the Pope] can do.

Third case. Jews commit offences not foreseen either by their Law or by the Christian Law. In this case, the inquisitor does not have to intervene, because it is not in his jurisdiction.

It happens that Jews are condemned to death and killed when they are struggling against the Christian faith. This happens when they resist the **conversion** of one of their own to Christianity, threatening him with stoning [for blasphemy] or actually stoning him. Jews guilty of this offence will be burnt and none of those who take part in such an act should escape the fire.

A Jew invokes the name of the Cross or crosses himself. One should always consider that he does this to show his contempt for the Christian religion.

May the inquisitor pursue Jews who, on Easter day, crucify a lamb or else stamp on the cross with their feet, to insult the faith? No. These Jews thus show their wish to injure the Christian faith, but to injure the faith is not to commit an error against it. Thus these offences do not concern the Office of the **Inquisition**, whose powers are perfectly delimited. But secular judges and ordinary ecclesiastical judges can constrain [these Jews], at least indirectly [*sic*] to abandon such practices.

Jews are obliged to accept evidence or charges brought against them by Christians. On the other hand, they are forbidden to bear witness against Christians.

A Jew who embraces the sect of the **Saracens** should not be punished, for the simple reason that ... the sect of the Jews is worse than that of the Saracens, and one shall not punish someone who abandons the worst of sects for a bad sect.

Let us now examine which practices are permitted to Jews who live among Christians.

They may have old [established] synagogues, and maintain and restore them, but they may not build new ones.

They may celebrate, in their synagogues, their festivals and regular services, [but] peacefully and without making a disturbance.

They may [normally] gather together with the Christians of their town and neighbourhood, but sometimes this may be forbidden to them.

Jews who respect the [Christian] law are not molested by Christians.

Violence is not done to them to force them to convert.

Without the sentence of a ruler, Jews must not be wounded or killed or despoiled of their goods.

They bury their own dead, and the bodies of their dead are not exhumed from their cemeteries.

All their rites are tolerated, in so far as the celebration of them does not constitute an offence to the Catholic faith. [The Jews] retain all the privileges which have been granted to them by the sovereign **pontiffs**.

But can the king or prince, without [himself] sinning, expel them from a town or from a kingdom? It has been said that they can, and it has been added that the king may seize [the Jews'] goods, and that the Pope may order this, even if he does not have to carry it out, if they create no scandal and if they live peacefully.

Up to now, Jews subjected to perpetual captivity, through their own fault, have benefited from Christian mercy, which has welcomed and nourished them. Up until our days, they have lived together with Christians. But today, the most Christian rulers of Castile, Aragon, Sicily and Granada have taken measure of their ingratitude. [The Jews] respond to the generosity of the Christians by seeking conflict with them, by imposing usury on them, by subverting numerous [Christian] faithful, whom they instruct in the Law of Moses and whom they initiate into their rights and ceremonies. Their activities are such, their dealings with Christians so familiar, that today the heretics and apostates who live in these kingdoms are legion.

Thus, to end this scandal, these most serene kings have expelled [the Jews] from their kingdoms and their lands. And they have shown proof of mercy, not of rigour, for they could have taken all their goods from them or had them executed. They could have had them all burnt like heretics, they could have had all their children forcibly baptized, despite [the will of] their parents, but they did not do so. The Jews have had centuries in which to amend their ways, and have done no such thing. They have remained faithful to their depraved customs despite all the time they have lived in the company of the [Christian] faithful. It is right that they should have been exiled from the kingdoms of the faithful. Their perversions were such that the rulers could in good conscience have had them all killed.

5. The Inquisition and Jewish converts in Spain

(a) The trial of Gonzalo Pérez Jarada: the case of the Toledo Inquisition's prosecutor against Gonzalo Pérez Jarada, councillor of Trujillo, in south-west Spain, in his trial, which took place in 1489-1490.

[From Haim Beinart, *Trujillo. A Jewish community in Extremadura on the eve of the expulsion from Spain* (=*Hispania Judaica*, vol. 2), Jerusalem, 1980, pp. 288-9; in Spanish]

I, Diego Martínez de Ortega, bachelor in decrees [of canon law], **procurator fiscal** in the Holy Inquisition in this most noble city of Toledo and all its archdiocese, appear before your reverences [the inquisitors], before whom, and for their judgement, I propose accusation against and accuse Gonzalo Pérez Jarada, **regidor** of the town of Trujillo, and citizen [*vecino*] of Illescas, who is present, that the same, living in the name and possession of Christian and calling himself such and enjoying the privileges and exemptions and liberties that Christians enjoy, is [in fact] in contempt of Holy Mother Church, a heretic and apostate from our Holy Catholic faith, following and keeping the Law of Moses and its rites and ceremonies. About this, being imprisoned in the town of Valladolid, in the gaol of the Holy Inquisition, and being much urged, and warned a number of times, he made his confession falsely, with dissimulation and deception, thinking in that way to be freed from temporal penalties and paying no regard to how he might pay those of eternity. He remained silent about and concealed the nature and seriousness of other greater [offences], thinking that they would remain secret and would not be discovered from [the evidence] of those which he had falsely confessed.

[Thus] he excused himself when he should have accused himself. None the less he stated that he once stayed in a Jewish house, and they gave him pieces of beef and veal and other bits of meat, and that he accepted and ate them, but not as a rite [*cirimonia*] of the Law of Moses. In the same way, he gave three yards of cloth to a Jew to make a robe. And he arranged for a sheep to be given for the wedding of a Jewess who was his guest. Also, he went to pay his respects at the weddings of certain Jews, because that is the custom in the town of Trujillo. Also, when he was ill, he ate meat on the Sabbath and ate Jewish fruit [*sic*], but not as a '**ceremony**'. Also, he gave some of his children's clothes to a Jewish peddler, because he asked for them. Also, on Friday night he went to dine with a Jew, and ate his bread and drank his wine, and not 'for ceremony'. And many times he went into the synagogue to call on many Jews and ask them for money, and settled his accounts with them [there]. Also, he had a Jewish servant boy who lived with him because another left. And he swore that he had not carried out any other 'ceremonies'.

All of which, that is, his simulated and deceiving confession, having been carefully examined by your reverences, appears to be deceiving, and not [made] with a pure heart, by a man who is so suspect. Also, he constantly conversed and dealt with Jews, and with other people who were involved in the aforesaid ceremonies [i.e. **conversos**]. It may be assumed, and objected against him that he did this in order to keep to the aforesaid Law of Moses. For that reason he remained silent concerning the incidents and ceremonies which he kept quiet about and concealed, and [matters] involving him which could not be forgotten, thinking that they would remain secret and would not be discovered, so that he might continue in his errors. And those matters about which he remained silent, and which he concealed, are as follows:

Item. Holding the said Law of Moses to be good, and having devotion to it and to its Synagogue, he gave a gown to a Jew so that [the latter] would undertake to pour oil into the synagogue lamp [which burns perpetually before the ark containing the scrolls of the Law of Moses], so that God would grant health to one of his sons, who was ill.

Also, [the accused], believing in the said Law of Moses, and that the things of the Synagogue were more to be honoured than those of Holy Mother Church, when he saw the scroll of the Law, humbled himself before it and gave it great reverence and respect.

Also, he refused to eat suffocated partridges [i.e. those killed by Christians], and ordered that they should be brought to him alive, and he had the throats of the meat he intended to eat slit with [Jewish] ceremony.

Also, on Friday afternoons the said Gonzalo Pérez would pray with bowing [*meldando*] like a Jew.

Also, he asked for a special Jewish prayer [*a pazu*] for one of his children whom he was worried about, and asked [the Jews] to come and read it to him, in which [action] he gave the appearance of denying the faith and truth of the Holy Gospels and of Holy Mother Church, and of believing in the ghost of the dead Law.

Also, he had **phylacteries** and asked for them so that he could put them on and take them about with him. And he made **booths** and went into them [for the Feast].

Also, he took part in *samas*, which is the great conversation and business that takes place at the lighting of the lamps in the synagogue.

And also, he ate meat during Lent, even though he was not ill, and this in the houses of Jews, [the meat] having been killed with [Jewish] ceremony. And he sent the birds he intended to eat to Jews to have their throats slit, and he did not eat bacon. And whenever he could he excused himself from eating anything which was forbidden by the Law of Moses.

And being regarded as guilty of the aforesaid offence of heresy, he was first summoned and cited as a heretic in the town of Plasencia. He did not present himself or appear before the Inquisitors who summoned and cited him, to save himself and make excuse for the infamy and offence which was being held and proved against him. And also, in order to comply more fully with the said Law of Moses, he fasted the Great Fast of the Jews [Yom Kippur], not eating until nightfall, and on that day he would ask pardon of others and they of him, and he heard the recitation of, and [himself] recited, prayers from the Law of Moses on the day of the Great Fast. And he has remained silent about and has hidden what he knew about other people who carried out the aforesaid ceremonies, being [himself] a heretic and apostate in other cases and matters, which have come to my notice, and which I [hereby] announce that I will declare and denounce during the progress of this summary process. By and through these same acts, rites and ceremonies, the aforesaid Gonzalo Pérez committed and perpetrated the crime and offence of heresy and apostasy, and [hence] is a heretic and an apostate, and has incurred the sentence of major excommunication and the confiscation and loss of all his goods, and all the other penalties and censures established in the laws against such heretics.

Thus I hereby ask and require you, most reverend sirs, to pronounce and declare the said Gonzalo Pérez to be indeed a heretic and apostate, and to have incurred the aforesaid sentences…. And I swear to God and on the sign of the Cross, and on the words of the Holy Gospels, that I do not bring forward this accusation maliciously, but because I am thus informed and because such denunciations have been made to me. And if I am bound to undertake any other solemn act, declaration or justification concerning [this matter], I am ready to do so, in so far as I can, and in no other manner.

(b) A Christian convert to Judaism tries to keep Jewish dietary laws: Spain, 1501. A pre-trial statement made to the Inquisition in Soria, on 9 February 1501, by Ana, wife of Juan de Fraguas, also of Soria, in which she claims to have observed concern about kosher law in a neighbour's kitchen.

[From Carlos Carrete Parrondo, ed., *El tribunal de la Inquisición en el obispado de Soria (1486-1502)*, *Fontes Iudæorum Regni Castellæ*, II Salamanca, 1985, p. 116; in Spanish]

Ana, wife of Juan de Fraguas, an inhabitant of Soria..., said that, perhaps five years ago ... this witness had as a neighbour Leonor, wife of Diego de Salinas, both 'New Christians', inhabitants of Soria, and, one day, the aforesaid Leonor put a pot on to cook in this witness's house, with water in it to cook meat. And this witness, when she [Leonor] was out of the room, thinking to do her a favour, put a little bacon into ... her pot. And before she could throw the meat into the pot, [Leonor] came back and when she saw the bacon, she turned the pot over so that the bacon fell on a bench and filled it with water again to carry on with the cooking.

6. A Venetian Jew on trial

The interrogation by Venetian inquisitors of Gian Giacomo *detto Simele* [the 'like one'], on 17 August 1558.

[From Pier Cesare Ioly Zorattini, *Processi del S. Uffizio di Venezia contro Ebrei e Giudaizzanti (1548-1560)*, Florence, 1980, vol. 1, pp. 279-281; in Italian]

Wednesday, 17th August 1558.

Ordered into the [Inquisitorial] office, the abovementioned Simile, the Jew, in continuation of his interrogation was asked, 'What reason made you be baptized and become a Christian?' He replied, 'Faith'. Asked who had instructed him in the faith, he replied, 'One Mr Mathio Gottich, a German doctor, who was a Jew and who practises in the house of the **Magnificent** Mr Andrea Pasqualigo, and who taught [the latter's] children Hebrew, Greek and Latin. He made me realize my error and enlightened me, in addition to which he read to me from the books [of the Law] and the Prophets. Also, I was taught by his excellency Mr Mathio de Riva, a lawyer. Thus I came to the [Christian] faith and had myself baptized.

Asked if he knows the Lord's Prayer, the **Hail Mary** and the **Creed**, he replied, 'Yes sir, and I say it [all] every morning'. Asked if he believes in our faith he replied, 'Yes sir, and for that reason I made myself a Christian and I wish to die in that faith'. It was said to him, 'If you made yourself a Christian in order to be a Christian, why did you continue so long in Judaism, and live a Jewish life, as you stated in the other [previous] interrogation?' He replied, 'I did it in order to bring my wife and my children, of whom I have two, one seven and the other five years old, and my sister named Richa, a maiden of seventeen, to the faith. For this reason I remained among the Jews and lived with them, but through it all I lived as the Christian which I am, and made my confession and received communion and went to **mass**. Asked, 'Did you go to these services in a yellow hat [the distinguishing mark of a Jew in Venice]?', he replied, 'No sir. I went out of the territory [of Venice] to Brescia, where I spent a fortnight and passed the festival of Christmas. I stayed in the house of Mr Marcello Ugo, and there I wore a black hat [that of a Christian], and accompanied Mr Piero Barbena, a lawyer, and went to Carpi, where I spent three or four days, and then went to Treviso....'

Asked, 'When were you baptized?', he replied, 'About three years ago'. Asked, 'During those three years, were your wife and your children in this land [of Venice]?', he replied, 'No sir'.... Asked to which tribe [of Israel] he belonged, he replied, 'I am of the tribe of **Levi**'. Asked if, in the synagogue, he did the office that is performed by the Levites in the synagogue, he replied, 'Not after I was baptized'. Warned that he should take care to speak the truth, he replied, 'It is not otherwise'. Of his own volition he said, 'I did [all this] in accordance with my baptismal licence, as the Magnificent Mr Andrea Pasqualigo said, so that I might bring [lit. 'reduce'] my children and my wife to the faith'. He said [to the inquisitor], without prompting... 'Sir, be sure that no Jew is interrogated against me, because I want to oppose such a thing, as they will come to ruin me if they find out that I am a Christian'.

This account was confirmed and [the prisoner] was returned to his cell.

7. Pope Julius III's attack on the Talmud

As the Counter-Reformation gets underway, Pope Julius III renews the papal attack on rabbinical Judaism which began three centuries earlier.

[From Simonsohn, *Documents*, dated at Rome, 29 May 1554, pp. 2920-1; in Latin]

[Pope Julius III] ... To all and each of the venerable brother patriarchs, archbishops and bishops and other our beloved sons who are **ordinaries** of **places**, greeting, etc.

We have recently received, and not without disturbance of our soul, from others of our venerable brothers, cardinals of the Holy Roman Church, who are inquisitors-general of heretical depravity in the universal Christian Republic, a certain quantity of Jewish books, called *Ghemarot Talmut*, containing certain improper things and material offensive to divine law and orthodox faith. This, by our order, was condemned and burned [by the inquisitors] in the fire.

Nevertheless, there are said to exist among these said Jews various books, which contain sundry **blasphemies** and insults against Christ our Redeemer, and his most holy name and honour. We [therefore], wishing to provide appropriately in the above case, hereby commit this matter to you and your men and order you to inform every one of the Jewish communities which live within the limits of our jurisdiction that, at the end of four months after the date of this intimation and notification, they should surrender each and every book in which the name of Jesus our Saviour, who is called in Hebrew 'Iesevi Hanozri', is named with blasphemy or otherwise insulted, whether in their synagogues and public places or in private houses, and that those who were found to be in possession of such books by whatever means are to be punished by due penalties, both financial, with the confiscation of goods, and, if their obstinacy and the nature of their offence requires it, punished without mercy, and corporally, even to the ultimate punishment [of death], and also by other penalties by which apostates from the faith of Christ are punished. And nevertheless, those four months having elapsed, either you yourselves or another or others whom you may depute for this [purpose], should with all diligence enquire into these books and examine them studiously, and have them enquired into and investigated. And those whom you find in possession of such books you should punish in every case and without fail, by means of the penalties with which the aforementioned apostates are punished. In addition, you must not permit those same Hebrews who are tolerated by Holy Mother Church as a memorial of the Lord's Passion, to be vexed or molested by [anyone] acting on apostolic [papal] authority, except by our express command, so that at some [future] time, attracted by our gentleness and by the breath of the Holy Spirit, they may be converted to the true light of Christ, [all this] provided that the books in their possession do not contain blasphemy.

II: Expulsion of Jews

The theme of this chapter is what appears to be called, in the 'modern' world, 'ethnic cleansing' These documents describe some of the actions which were taken, in various European states, and particularly in the Iberian peninsula, as well as Bohemia (now part of the Czech Republic) and Italy, to remove the Jewish presence from their communities. The story begins with the reaction of the king of Castile, Henry III, to the attacks on all the major Jewish communities in the kingdom. After the event, the king ordered the punishment of the ringleaders, but, in the succeeding decades, many Spanish Jews converted to Christianity. Although the letter translated here was addressed specifically to the city council in Burgos, it is typical of royal reaction to the killing and robbery of Jews elsewhere in Castile and in the neighbouring kingdom of Aragon.

A document issued by Benedict XIII, who was recognised as pope in much of Iberia for a number of years but eventually emerged as an 'anti-pope', indicates that the idea of expulsion, which had already been tried out elsewhere in Europe, was being at least considered in the kingdom of Castile, nearly ninety years before the 1492 edict of expulsion, which is also included here. Ferdinand's instruction to the Inquisitor-general Tomás de Torquemada, which he issued later that year in his capacity as king of Aragon, appears to give substance to the view that the edict of March 31 was aimed more at the conversion than the expulsion of the Jews of Castile and Aragon. This interpretation is further confirmed by the document which was issued in Barcelona in November 1492, which offered to restore their property to Jews who returned to the kingdoms of the Catholic Monarchs as baptised Christians. The mental state of those who departed, and of the Jewish Christians, the conversos, *who remained, are represented by the comments of the Andalusian priest-chronicler, Andrés Bernáldez, and by extracts from the trials of the self-proclaimed prophetess Inés de Herrera and of the* converso *preacher, Alonso de Córdoba Membreque. Estimates vary concerning the number of Spanish Jews who departed in 1492, and it is even harder to gauge how many returned as baptised Christians in that and succeeding years.*

In the second section of this chapter, the focus shifts to Portugal. The Christian chronicler Damião de Gois gives a graphic description of the combined mass baptism and expulsion of that country's Jews, while Spanish records indicate the mental state of some of those who chose to take up the

Crown's offer of a return to their old lives, but in a new guise, as Christians. In Portugal, 'New Christians' had to suffer a massacre in Lisbon in 1506, again vividly described by Gois. In some respects, though, the poetry of Portuguese Jewish converts to Christianity, with its deep involvement in the theme of Jewish liberation, perhaps best expresses the painful dilemmas which faced both departed and returned converts, and two examples of such poets' work are included here. Meanwhile, as Jews and converts found themselves wandering around Europe, and in particular the Mediterranean, the rabbis outside the Iberian peninsula were faced with the problem of deciding whether those who avowed their intention of returning to Judaism could be treated as Jews. Opinions on this question, delivered before and after 1492, give a thorough treatment of the issues involved.

The chapter concludes with examples of expulsion decrees from other parts of Europe, where such measures had local rather than national effect. This was because of the fragmented political map in some other European countries, such as Italy and Germany. For those involved, of course, the disruption and suffering were great. The overall effect was to remove Jews and their community life from much of western Europe by 1500, though some Jews began to return in the latter part of the sixteenth century.

Spanish persecutions and expulsions

8. Pogroms in Spain, 1391

Letter from Henry III of Castile to Burgos city council concerning a recent **pogrom**, 16 June 1391.

[From Fritz [Yitzhak] Baer, *Die Juden im christlichen Spanien*, Berlin, 1929, 1936, repr. 1970, vol. 2, pp. 252-3; in Spanish]

Understand that it has become known how, in the last few days, in the most noble cities of Seville and Córdoba, through inducements and persuasion exercised by the archdeacon of Ecija, some of the lesser people of the said cities, behaving like troublemakers and men of little understanding, without thought for our interests and our [prerogative? and not] fearing God or my justice, or considering the situation I am in or my age [he was a minor], attacked the Jews living in the **aljamas** of the said towns, killed some of them, robbed others and forced others to become Christians.

As a result, the Jews who used to live in these communities have been driven out, about which I am very angry, because this does me great disservice. And I, with my Council, have ordered [a commission] to be sent ... to investigate this event and by which person or persons it was started, and to do such great justice with them, and punish them so severely, that they should be an example to all who hear of it. They should be punished so that no-one [else] may have such wicked and ugly temerity as to go out against these Jews, in such a wicked way, knowing that [the Jews] were always guarded and defended by the kings, my ancestors; and the Church itself, according to its law, ordered them to be guarded and defended.

Wherefore, having seen this my letter, I order you, each and every one, to remedy this matter at once, and to have it publicly announced in this said city [of Burgos] that nobody at all should dare to act or move against Jews in general or against any one of them, to do them any annoyance or damage or injustice. You are to proceed at once with judicial remedies, giving such people signal justice and punishment, so that it may be a chastisement [even] to those who hear of it. And it is necessary that you should put this into operation at once, and not place a lengthy delay upon it ... and act in such a way that you give a good account of the said city [of Burgos] and of the Jews of that Jewry, as your ancestors did to those [kings] from whom I am descended, since as this city is the Head city [*cabeza*] of Castile, all [other] places will be calmed by the calm you impose in that city.

9. Local expulsion from Toro, 1404

'Anti-pope' Benedict XIII, bull dated 30 January 1404, from Tarrascon in the diocese of Avignon.

[From Shlomo Simonsohn, *The Apostolic See and the Jews: Documents: 1394–1464*, Toronto, 1989, no. 515, pp. 566–7; in Latin]

To Alfonso de Illescas, bishop of Zamora, salutation and **apostolic** blessing. Although the stubborn perfidy of the Jews is held not undeservedly as despicable by devotees of true religion and orthodoxy, because we are sure that nonetheless the remnant of prophetic witness is eventually to be saved and added to the children of the Catholic Church, [and] also because they bear the image of God, the authority of the Apostolic See has judged that they are not to be eliminated [*sic*] from Christian territories, but out of humane duty should live among these same [Christian] faithful, and similarly permits them to carry out the rites and ceremonies of their Law, without harm to our faith.

[According to a subsequent phrase in this document, 'The Jews of the aforesaid town were expelled', though a document in Baer, *Die Juden*, vol. 2, pp. 252-6, records that the abbot gave a grant at this time for the building of a new synagogue in Toro]

10. Expulsion edict, 1492

[From Luis Suárez Fernández, *Documentos acerca de la expulsión de los Judíos*, Valladolid, 1964, pp. 392-3; in Spanish]

Don Ferdinand and Doña Isabella, by the grace of God king and queen of Castile, of León, of Aragon [etc.]. To Prince John, our most dear and most beloved son, and to the other royal children, prelates, dukes, marquises, counts, masters of the [**military**] **orders**, priors [etc.], and to the town councils, **corregidores**, [etc.] of the most noble and most loyal city of Burgos and of the other archdioceses, bishoprics and dioceses of our kingdoms and lordships and to the communities of Jews of the aforesaid city of Burgos ... and of all the other cities and towns and villages of that diocese and of all the other cities and towns and villages of our aforementioned kingdoms and lordships and to all the Jews and individual members of [those communities], men as well as women, of whatever age they may be, and to all other persons of whatever law, estate, dignity and preeminence and condition they may be, who are or may be affected in any way by what is written below in this our letter, salutation and grace.

You well know, or should know, that because we were informed that in these our kingdoms there were certain bad Christians who judaised and apostasised from our holy Catholic faith, for which much of the reason was the communication by the Jews with the Christians, in the parliament [*cortes*] that we caused to happen in the city of Toledo in the former year of 1480, we ordered that, in all the cities and towns and villages of our kingdoms and lordships, the Jews should be separated out where they lived, hoping that with their separation [*apartamiento*] the problem would be solved. Also we had procured and ordered that an Inquisition should be made in our aforesaid kingdoms and lordships, which, as you know, was done more than twelve years ago and is still going on. It has discovered many guilty people, as is well known, and as we are informed by the inquisitors and by many religious people, ecclesiastical and secular, a great danger to Christians has clearly emerged, this having followed, and still continuing, from the activity, conversation [and] communication which [these Christians] have maintained with Jews. [These Jews] demonstrate that they always work, by whatever ways and means they can, to subvert and remove faithful Christians from our holy Catholic faith, to separate them from it, and attract and pervert [them] to their wicked belief and opinion, instructing them in the ceremonies and observances of their Law.

They organise meetings at which they read to them and teach them what they have to believe and observe according to their Law, succeeding in circumcising them and their sons, giving them books from which they recite their prayers, and announcing to them the fasts they have to fast and joining with them to read and to teach them the stories of their Law, notifying them of the great festivals [*pascuas*] before they arrive, informing them of what they have to observe and do in [these festivals]. They give [to the Christians] and bring to their houses unleavened bread and ritually slaughtered meat, instructing them in the things from which they must abstain, both foodstuffs and other things for the observance of their Law, and persuade them, in so far as they can, to keep and guard the Law of Moses, making them to understand that there is no other law or truth except that one. This is evident from many statements and confessions, both by the Jews themselves and by those who were perverted and deceived by them, all of which has resulted in great harm and detriment to, and opprobrium of, our Holy Catholic Church.

Seeing that we were informed of much of this before now, and that we know that the true remedy for all these injuries was to reduce to nothing communication between the said Jews and the Christians, and throw them out of all our kingdoms, we desired to content ourselves with ordering them to leave all the cities, towns and villages of Andalusia, where it seemed that they had done the most damage, believing that would be enough to stop [the Jews] of the other cities and towns of our kingdoms and lordships from doing the above. We are informed that neither that [measure] nor the judicial acts which have been carried out against some of the said Jews, who have been found most culpable of the said crimes and offences against our holy Catholic faith, are enough to be a complete remedy. For this reason and to avoid and put an end to so great a shame and offence to the Christian faith and religion, because every day it is found and becomes apparent that the said Jews increasingly pursue their bad and wicked project wherever they live and have converse [with Christians], and so that there should be no further occasion for offence to our holy faith, among those whom God has so far chosen to keep safe, as well as those who fell, amended their ways and returned to Holy Mother Church, which [danger], given the weakness of our human nature and the devil's cunning and suggestion, continually and at every opportunity warring against us, could happen, if the principal cause of all this is not removed, [means we have] to throw the said Jews out of our kingdoms.

Because, when some grave and detestable crime is committed by members of some college and university, it is right that such a **college** and **university** should be dissolved and annihilated and the lesser members punished by the greater, and the ones [punished] by the others. Also, those who pervert the good and honest living of cities and towns, and may damage others by contagion, should be expelled, and this even for lighter causes which may be a danger to the republic. Even more so for the most dangerous and contagious of crimes such as this.

Therefore we, with the counsel and opinion of certain prelates and **grandees** and knights of our kingdoms, and of other persons of knowledge and understanding in our Council, after much deliberation about [the matter], agree to order all the Jews and Jewesses of our kingdoms to leave, and never return or come back to them, or any one of them. And in this matter we order this our letter to be given, by which we give order to all Jews and Jewesses of whatever age they may be, who live and dwell in our aforesaid kingdoms and lordships, both those native to them and non-natives, by whatever means and for whatever reason they have come and may reside within them, that by the end of the month of July coming, in this current year, they should leave all our aforesaid kingdoms and lordships, with their sons and daughters, Jewish menservants and maidservants and household members, great or small, of whatever age they may be, and that they should not dare to return to them or reside in them, nor in any part of them, for dwelling or passage or in any other way, on pain that, if they fail to do thus and comply, and are found to have been in our aforesaid kingdoms and lordships and to have come into them by any means, they may incur the penalty of death and confiscation of all their goods for our **Chamber** and **Exchequer**, which penalties they may incur in accordance with this same act and law without further process, sentence or declaration.

And we give orders and forbid that any person at all in our aforesaid kingdoms, of whatever estate, condition or dignity they may be, should dare to receive or welcome or defend or guard publicly or secretly, any Jew or Jewess, from the said term of the end of July, henceforth for evermore, whether in their lands, or their houses or in any other part of our kingdoms and lordships, on pain of the loss of all their goods, vassals and fortresses and other properties, and also the loss of any grants that they may hold from us through our Chamber and Exchequer.

And so that the said Jews and Jewesses may, during the said interval up to the end of the said month of July, better dispose of themselves and of their goods and property, by this present we take and receive them under our security and protection and royal defence, and we secure them and their goods, so that, during this time up to the aforesaid end of the said month of July, they may walk and be secure and may enter and sell and exchange and transfer to others all their movable and immovable goods, and dispose of them freely and at their will, and that during this time no harm or damage or illegal act should be done to their persons or goods, against justice, under the penalties those who break our royal safe conduct fall into and incur. Also we give licence and faculty to the said Jews and Jewesses to take their goods and property out of all our said kingdoms and lordships, by sea and by land, provided that they do not take out gold and silver or minted coins, or the other things forbidden [for export] by the laws of our kingdoms.

11. Jews convert

The Inquisitor-general, and prior of Santa Cruz in Avila, Tomás de Torquemada, is ordered by Ferdinand, to collect reports from his subordinate inquisitors in both kingdoms, Castile and Aragon, concerning earlier 'errors' (lapses into their former faith) by Jews who decided to convert to Christianity after the issue of the expulsion edict for unbaptised Jews [see 10 above]. Dated at Santa Fe, near Granada, 15 May 1492.

[From *La expulsión de los Judíos de la Corona de Aragón. Documentos para su estudio*, ed. Rafael Conde and Delgado de Molina, Zaragoza, 1991, p. 179; in Spanish]

The king

Venerable and devout Father Prior. I have been informed that, since the banishment of the Jews was published, some of them, indeed many, wish to be Christians, but are afraid to do this because of the Inquisition, believing that, for a minor offence which they may [previously] have committed, they will suffer a severe penalty. This frightens them very much, and they do not dare [to convert], unless this situation is remedied in some way. And because it is right to ensure that those souls are saved which would otherwise be lost, I and the most serene queen, my dear and beloved wife, decided to ask for the opinion of our Council [whether the reference was to the Royal Council of Castile or to the Supreme Council of the Inquisition, which was established in 1483 and covered both the Catholic Monarchs' kingdoms is not clear, though the latter seems more probable] on the matter. They have told us it seems to them that there is no better remedy than that you should write to the inquisitors and to the officials of the Inquisition in all our kingdoms and lordships, ordering them that, although there may be some action [initiated] against those persons who may have converted in this way and become Christians, after their expulsion [if they remained as Jews] was announced, they should not take action against them, but rather the information or testimony which may have been provided against [these converts] should be sent to you, so that the aforesaid Council may see it and provide for whatever fulfils the service of God, so that they may be sure that no such harm will be done to them, or at least that they should not be harmed by [inquisitorial] excesses, and should not be injured unjustly.

All this seemed good to us. Therefore, I request and charge you that, since this, which you now see, is in the service of our Lord, and from it follows little damage to the [**Holy**] **Office**, you should determine to provide in this way at once, writing on the subject, in the best possible manner, to all the officials [of the Inquisition], so that they may act on and carry out all the above, for doing so will be a service to God, and [also] you will give me much pleasure and service.

Given in the town of Santa Fe on 15 May 1492

12. The Jews depart from Spain, 1492

A comment by a contemporary chronicler

[From Andrés Bernáldez, *Memorias de los reyes católicos*, ed. M. Gómez-Moreno and J. de M. Carriazo (Madrid, 1962), p. 254; in Spanish]

The rich Jews paid the exit price for the poor Jews and they treated one another in that departure with great charity. So that in no manner did they want to convert, except for some, who were very few, of those in the greatest need. The Jews at that time, whether simple [*sic*] or lettered, commonly held the opinion and all believed, wherever they lived, that just as with a strong hand and outstretched arm and with much honour and wealth, God through Moses had miraculously taken out the other people of Israel from Egypt, so too from these parts of

Spain they would return and depart with much honour and riches, without losing anything of their own, to possess the Holy Promised Land, which they confessed to having lost because of their great and abominable sins which their ancestors had committed against God. Concerning which, in this departure, the total opposite of what they expected took place, because they were deniers and enemies of the truth.

For in the other Exodus, in which they came out from captivity in Egypt, by command of our Lord who was their Saviour and loved them well, in return for the labours and scourges which the Egyptians had given them and promised them, He commanded them to rob Egypt with impunity: and they robbed it when they decided to depart and go into the wilderness, wherever God commanded them. Saying that they would return, they asked to borrow gold and silver jewels, silk and cloth and other things from the Egyptians, which they lent them and which [the Jews] kept, as the twelfth chapter of the [book of Exodus] says. And at that time this was no discredit to them, for they were good and humble and believed in God, sovereign and eternal, and the Egyptians were evil and unbelieving and idolaters and not sons of Israel but sons of Canaan and of perdition. And [now] the Christians are good, and sons of the Law and blessing and obedience, and people of God and sons of Israel, since from the people of Israel they had the beginning of salvation, and had the law and knew and received the true Messiah who redeemed them, who was our Redeemer Jesus Christ, God and man, whom God had promised to send and [duly] sent; whom they, through their malice, did not recognise or receive at that time, nor did they wish to give him a hearing of the great miracles and marvels that he did. Instead, with malice they persecuted him and killed him.

In the six months' period of the edict, they sold and virtually gave away whatever they could of their estates. Young and old prepared themselves for the journey, demonstrating great courage and hope of having a prosperous departure and great happenings. And in everything they had perverse misfortunes. For Christians took their many estates, very many rich houses and landed properties for a few coins, and [the Jews] went about begging to sell them, but they could not find anyone to buy them. They exchanged a house for an ass, and a vineyard for a small piece of cloth or linen, because they could not take out either gold or silver. But it is true that they secretly took out an infinite amount of gold and silver [in coin], which they swallowed and carried out in their bellies through those customs posts in which they had to be searched, and in the ports, both inland and beside the sea. The women, in particular, swallowed more; a person might swallow thirty ducats at one time.

13. An offer of return, 1492

Barcelona, 10 November 1492

[From Suárez Fernández, *Documentos*, pp. 487-9, in Spanish]

Don Ferdinand and Doña Isabella, [etc],

Know that on the part of some Jews, residing in the kingdom of Portugal, who by our command departed from our kingdoms and lordships, an account has been given of how they, illuminated by the Holy Spirit, realising the error in which they were, wanted to return to these our kingdoms to convert to our holy Catholic faith and remain and die in it as Catholic Christians, and that, at their petition, it was supplicated and asked of us as a grace that, in order that they might come to these our kingdoms, we should give them our letter of safe-conduct, so that they might return freely and securely to them, with their children and wives and property. And thus, because their will was to live and die in the same places in which they lived and dwelt when they were Jews, we should command that the houses and goods and property which they sold and abandoned should be restored and returned to them by the people who hold them now, for the quantities of **maravedis** for which they sold them, paying for improvements that might have been made in them, or as our pleasure might be.

And we, favouring the above as being to the service of our Lord and the exaltation of our holy Catholic faith, found it to be good and ordered this letter to be given and gave it, concerning this matter. Whereby we take and receive, under our royal protection and defence, all the Jews and Jewesses who may wish to come to our said kingdoms and lordships, having first turned Christian [*sic*] in ... Ciudad Real or in the said kingdom of Portugal, or else becoming Christians and receiving water of the Holy Spirit in the first place [they came to] inside our kingdoms, that is to say, those who leave Portugal via Badajoz should become Christians in the said city of Badajoz, and those who leave via Ciudad Rodrigo should become Christians in Ciudad Rodrigo, and those who leave via the city of Zamora should become Christians in the said city of Zamora. And that in whichever of the aforesaid cities they may be baptised, they should be baptised in the presence of the bishop or of his vicar-general or the *corregidor* or magistrates of the city and they should carry an authentic certificate that they received baptism in the above manner. Similarly, we command that such a certificate should be carried by those who convert in the said kingdom of Portugal and may wish to enter our aforesaid kingdoms, so that we may be certain how the said Jews became Christians, and there may be no trick or pretence in it at all. And we protect the said Jews who are in the said kingdom of Portugal and who may wish to become Christians in [our kingdoms], if they come via the aforesaid towns and through any one of them, so that they benefit from what is contained in this letter, and not [if they come] by any other route.

In the case of these people, and the goods they may bring with them, we give them protection against all or any persons of whatever law, estate or condition, pre-eminence or dignity they may be, so that no evil or harm or injustice at all should be done to them, in their persons or in their aforesaid goods and wealth, against reason and law and as ought not to be done. And we order you our … justices, each and every one of you, in your **places** and jurisdictions, to observe and comply with this our letter of safe-conduct, and have it observed and complied with, for the aforesaid Jews who thus come to our said kingdoms having become Christians, or who become Christians within our said kingdoms, and bear evidence to it in the abovementioned form, in every respect and by every means, according to what is contained within it, and against its tenor and form you should not go or pass or allow [others] to go at any time or in any way.

And we hereby command you that, whenever you are so requested by the aforesaid Jews who become Christians in this way, you should summon before you the persons to whom they sold their aforesaid houses and estates, at the time when they departed and went from these our kingdoms. When you find out from them the quantities of *maravedis* for which they sold them, and when they have been paid back for the improvements that they may have made to them, you should have them freely returned and restored [to their original owners], so that [these people] may exist and live freely in their said houses and estates, without any impediment being placed in their way, since it is our grace and will that things should be done and carried out thus. Similarly, if any persons used to owe [the former Jews] any debt, you should ensure that such [debts] which are found to be just and proper are repaid, as long as they are not usurious or for [unjust] gain, or such that the laws of our kingdoms intend and dispose that they should not be paid.

14. Messianism among Jewish Christians

A witness's statement to the Toledo tribunal of the Inquisition: testimony of Juan de Segovia at the trial of Inés de Herrera, May 1500, about an outbreak of **Messianism**.

[From Baer, *Die Juden*, ii, pp. 528-9; in Spanish]

I admit my fault that ... perhaps fourteen months ago I went from [Toledo] to buy some leather [**cordovanes**] ... and while approaching the city.... I found one Lope Donoso ... and he said to me: 'A marvel happened this past night. The daughter of Juan Esteban went up to heaven, taken by an angel, and there she saw those who were in pain [in **purgatory**] and [those] in glory, and other things which he told me, which they would describe to me in greater detail there in the town. Overcome by what this person said to me, I strove to find out the truth of it, how it happened and what it was, and went to Juan Esteban, the father of the girl, and repeated what the above person had said to me ... and [asked Juan] to tell me the truth. The said Juan Esteban told me that what I had been told was the truth, and that in order to be more certain of it, I should do the necessary business,... [then] 'my aforesaid daughter will tell you about it at length and clearly', as indeed happened, and thus, as I was carrying out my business transactions in the square, the aforesaid Juan Esteban said to me that we should go to his house to talk to ... his daughter, and that I should ask ... the girl to tell me what had happened to her and how she went up to heaven'. She was somewhat embarrassed, and her father Juan Esteban said to her, 'Daughter, tell him the whole truth, how it happened'.

And then the girl told me how her mother, who was already dead, came there and took her by the hand and told her not to be afraid, because it was God's will that she should go up to heaven and see its secrets and see wonderful things. And at that moment her other hand was taken by another, a boy, who had died a few days before, and the angel was flying around them, and in this way she said that they took her up to heaven, where she saw purgatory and the souls who were suffering in it, and in the same way how, in another remote part [of heaven] there were others on golden chairs, in glory. In the same way she told me that, while she was there, in another place higher up, it seemed to her that there was much marble, and she asked the angel who it was speaking up there, and the angel said, 'Friend of God, those who are speaking up there are the ones who were burnt here on earth [by the Inquisition], who are there in glory. In the same way she saw angels of three kinds and other things she told me about which I cannot remember.

Thus I was left in such confusion and disturbance that I could not decide what was the truth or what I should believe. Among the other things that the aforesaid girl told me was that she had asked the angel to give her a sign, so that what she said would be believed, and that the angel replied that he would bring her a letter from the Lord. And as I was incredulous and not a little disturbed, I asked Juan Esteban to let me know when they brought this letter to his daughter, or anything else new offered itself. And having come back to my house in [Toledo], I stated and recounted all the above, as it had happened, to my wife and, while we were disturbed ... not knowing how to decide what was the truth..., Luis Guantero, citizen of the town of Herrera, came to this city ... and while I was talking with him ... he told me how the things that the girl and her father told me were increasing every day, because they were taking her up to heaven once each week. I asked him if she had brought back any sign from heaven. He told me there were three: one was a really large ear of grain, one was an olive and the other a little letter [*cartica*]. And one should not doubt this any more than one doubted God, and [only] those who were beyond salvation would not believe in it, that is to keep the law and believe in the Law of Moses, and that there was reason to fast, because in that land of Herrera everyone was doing it, even seven or eight year old children were being made to fast, and no-one bothered about his or her property, because they held it to be most certain, and so those with wealth gave to those without, with that same hope of being carried to the Promised Land, and that God had made a most excellent city in heaven, which was to be translated to earth, where all the *conversos* were to dwell and live in great abundance, lacking nothing ... And overcome by [Luis's] reasonings, I believed the above, and fasted for some days in the Jewish manner.

15. Trial of a Messianic Jew

Evidence of Mina, a Muslim slave of Juan de Córdoba de las Membrezas known as 'El Membreque', given on 28 July 1502, in a trial conducted by the Córdoba tribunal of the Inquisition, which was related to the earlier trial in Toledo (see document 14).

[From Rafael Gracia Boix, *Colección de documentos para la historia de la Inquisición de Córdoba* (Córdoba, 1981), pp. 31-3; in Spanish]

The aforesaid Mina said and deposed, declared and confessed the following: that for about two and a half years up to this date, she knows that she saw how **Bachelor** Alonso de Córdoba Membreque used to enter, and entered many times, the house of the said parish councillor [*jurado*] Juan de Córdoba de las Membrezas, this witness's master, being the cousin of her master, son of his brother, and that, from the times in which this witness saw him enter there, she knows that she saw how for the space of more or less four months the said Bachelor Alonso de Córdoba Membreque was accustomed to enter and entered a chamber [*palacio*] which is in the house of her aforesaid master, twice a week, to preach to Juan de Córdoba Membreque, merchant, citizen of this city of Córdoba, and to many other people mentioned in her confession, and that the days on which he preached were Monday and Thursday of each week and on those days, both the said Bachelor Alonso de Córdoba Membreque and all the other people who heard his sermons, fasted the fasts of the Jews, not eating all day until nightfall when the stars appeared, and she saw that when he went out to speak and preach each sermon, the said Bachelor Membreque stripped and took off his gown and used to put on and wear a white shirt over his doublet and put a cloth [**prayer-shawl?**] over his head. This cloth was white and had four white ribbons, one at each corner of the cloth.

When he preached on Thursdays, because he said it was the great fast, the Bachelor put white linen shoes on his feet, and when he preached on Mondays he took off his boots and shoes and thus barefooted he would get up, dressed in the abovementioned fashion, onto a chest, on which was placed an altar cloth, with a pair of [**missal?**] cushions upon it, and that the shirt that the said bachelor wore went down to his feet, the sleeves being puffed out and their mouths narrow [as in bishops' dress at the time]. Also that in all the said preachings she saw and heard how the said Bachelor Alonso de Córdoba Membreque would start to preach and speak from a book which he held in his hands at the time, and that he preached and spoke to the said Juan de Córdoba Membreque, and to all the other people who were present there [contained in her confession] that **Elijah** was to come to take all the *conversos* out of captivity and lead them to the Promised Land. [To prepare] for such a day, and so that what they desired should be accomplished sooner, all those present, and all the *conversos*, should fast the fasts of the Jews, not eating all day until nightfall, when the stars appeared, and that there, in the Promised Land, cousins would marry each other, and that great riches were prepared for them, and that on their way they would find a river of milk and another river of water, and that in one of these all the *conversos* would bathe, and that everyone, young or old, would become twenty-five years old. Bachelor Membreque read many other things from this book, in which it was said that the earth would tremble at the time when Elijah came to take them away, and that the heavens would open and the sun and the moon would die and that the sea would turn to blood and that the trees would dry up and that a great storm of stones would come, and in this way all the houses would be destroyed and everything razed to the ground. And that a great river would come, which would carry away all the riches that the *conversos* left behind [in Spain], so that the **Old Christians** would not enjoy them, and that all these earthquakes and miracles would be done by Elijah, so that all the *conversos* would believe in him and see the wonders he did and so that he would be king.... And that after these upheavals had happened, Elijah would come in the figure of an angel and would ask all the *conversos* whether they believed properly in the law of the Jews, and if they had believed in the law of the Christians, he would absolve them so that they came back to believe in the law of the Jews, because if they did not believe in it, they could not travel to the Promised Land. Also he would ask them which Jewish prayers they knew and how they recited them, in order to know of them if they were firm in the beliefs of the Jews, and that then, those who believed properly in the said law of the Jews and were firm in it he would strip of all their clothes and have them dressed in shining white garments, without any colour at all, but all white [with] white stockings.

They would take up lighted candles in their hands, and he would take them in procession through the cities and towns and villages where there were *conversos,* in the sight of all the world, and in the midst of all the cities and towns and villages Elijah would preach, in such a way that all the Old Christians would be converted to the law of the Jews, and then [Elijah] would take all the *conversos* with him to the Promised Land, and in the midst of the way, there was a cave from which would emerge the young *conversos* who were in the Promised Land, and they would marry all the girls who were available there for marriage, and on their way to the Promised Land they would eat nothing but unleavened bread and another bread, which should be made with a flour called **coscoja**.

Portuguese persecutions and expulsions

16. Expulsion

An account by a contemporary chronicler

[From Damião de Gois, *Cronica do felicissimo Rei Don Manuel*, in *Damião de Gois*, ed. Antonio Alvaro Doria, Lisbon, 1944, pp. 53-6; in Portuguese]

Many of the Jews born in the kingdom [of Portugal] and of those who came from Castile received the water of baptism, and those who did not want to convert then began to arrange matters suitably for their embarkation. At this time the king, for reasons that moved him thus, ordered that on a certain day their sons and daughters, aged fourteen and below, should be taken from them and distributed among the towns and villages of the kingdom, where at his own expense [the king] ordered that they should be brought up and indoctrinated in the faith of our saviour Jesus Christ. This was agreed by the king with his council of state in Estremoz, and from there he went to Evora at the beginning of Lent in the year 1497, where he announced that the appointed day would be Easter Sunday.

Because there was less secrecy among the members of the [royal] council than had been expected, concerning what had been ordered in this matter, on the day on which [this] was to happen, it was necessary for the king to command that the execution of this order should be implemented at once throughout the kingdom, before by means and devices the Jews might have sent their children abroad. This action was the cause, not only of great terror, mixed with many tears, pain and sadness among the Jews, but also of much fright and surprise among the Christians, because no [human] creature ought to suffer or endure having his children forcibly separated from him. And [even] among foreigners [perhaps the native population of Portugal's colonies] virtually the same feeling exists by natural communication [i.e. without Christianity], principally among the rational ones, because with them Nature communicates the effects of her law more freely than with irrational beasts.

This same law compelled many of the 'old' Christians to be so moved to pity and mercy by the angry cries, weeping and wailing of the fathers and mothers from whom their children were forcibly taken, that they themselves hid [Jewish children] in their houses so that [the Jews] should not see them snatched from their hands. Those [Christians] saved them, knowing that they were thus acting against the law and the pragmatic of their king and lord, and that this same natural law made the Jews themselves use such cruelty that many of them killed their children, by suffocating them and drowning them in wells and rivers, as well as other methods, preferring to see them die in this way rather than be separated from them, without hope that they would ever see them again; and, for the same reason, many of [the parents] killed themselves.

While these actions were being carried out, the king never ceased to concern himself with what was necessary for the salvation of these people's souls, so that, moved by piety, he played a trick on them, by ordering them to be allowed to embark. Of the three ports of the kingdom that were designated for this, he forbade them two and commanded that they should all go to Lisbon to embark, giving them the [quarter of] the Estaos in which to shelter, and more than twenty thousand souls gathered there. Because of these delays, the time that the king had fixed for their departure went by, and thus they all remained as captives. Finding themselves in so wretched a state, many of them placed themselves at the mercy of the king. He returned their children to them and promised them that for twenty years he would inflict no harm upon them and that they would become Christians; [all of] which the king conceded to them, together with many other privileges that he gave them. As for those who did not want to be Christians, he ordered immediate embarkation to be granted to them, thus freeing them from the captivity in which they found themselves; and they all passed over to the lands of the **Moors**.

Now it appears that we might be regarded as neglectful if we did not state the reason why the king ordered the children of the Jews to be taken from them, but not those of the Moors, because they too left the kingdom because they did not wish to receive the water of baptism and believe what the Catholic Church believes. The reason was that from the seizure of the Jews' children no harm could result for the Christians dispersed throughout the world, in which the Jews, because of their sins, do not have kingdoms or lordships, cities and towns, but rather, everywhere they live they are pilgrims and taxpayers, without having power or authority to carry out their wishes against the injuries and evils which are done to them. But for *our* sins and punishment, God allows the Moors to occupy the greater part of Asia and Africa and a great part of Europe, where they have empires and kingdoms and great lordships, in which many Christians are under tribute to them, as well as many whom they hold as captives. For all these [reasons], it would be very prejudicial to take the Moors' children way from them, because it is clear that they would not hesitate to avenge those to whom such an injury was done on the Christians living in the lands of other Moors, once they found out about it, and above all on the Portuguese, against whom they would have a particular grievance in this regard. And this was the reason why [the Muslims] were allowed to leave the kingdom with their children and the Jews were not, to all of whom God permitted through his mercy to know the way of truth, so that they might be saved in it.

17. Returnees and the converts' malaise: the case of Gonzalo de Vargas

The nostalgia of many Spanish Jews for the country from which they found themselves exiled in 1492 led some to return as baptised Christians. This was not, however, to be the end of their problems. Some of the complexities of the situation of individuals and families emerge from the records of the Inquisition.

[From *Fontes Iudæorum Regni Castellae*, iv, *Los judeoconversos de Almazán, 1501-1505. Origen familiar de los Lainez*, eds Carlos Carrete Parrondo and Carolina Fraile Conde, Salamanca, 1987, pp. 112-14; in Spanish]

(a) First witness [Sigüenza, 7 April 1501]

Pedro de Ledesma, painter, a dweller in ... Almazán, a sworn witness [etc.], said that perhaps a month and a half ago ... being ... one day in the house of Martín de Gómara..., and being his guest at the hearth, Gonzalo de Vargas, a **New Christian**, citizen of the said town, came there and they began to discuss some things concerning the faith; and then the said Gonzalo Vargas said, 'Oh, if only there was someone here who could understand me!', and this witness said to him, 'What do you mean, I don't understand you? I can't work it out'. And Gonzalo de Vargas said, 'If evil has come to us, we deserve it, since we didn't do the ceremonies or the things we were supposed to do. That's why this banishment came to us'. And then this witness said, 'Forget all about that. That Law is and was lost. No-one was saved by it; and our law of grace is such that all the world was saved in it'. And then ... Gonzalo de Vargas said, 'Has anyone come back from there [the other world]?'.

(b) Second witness [Sigüenza, n.d. 1501]

Another witness says that certain people were talking about whether no Moor [*sic*] or Jew had been saved before the coming of Christ, but only those who believed in him, and this witness says that he heard ...

Gonzalo de Vargas reply to this that this [expulsion] came to them because they did not keep the **Sabbath** or light candles. And he was told that all [the Jews] were lost [before] and that now he was in the Law of **Grace**. Our Lord would have mercy on all of those who believe in the Law of Jesus Christ, and to this Gonzalo de Vargas replied [asking] if anyone had come back from [the other world] so that [they could] know which was the better Law.

(c) Third witness [Almazán, 2 June 1505]

Pero Casero, citizen of Almazán, said that perhaps ten years ago, this witness and Gonzalo de Vargas, a New Christian and labourer, citizen of Almazán, and others whom he cannot remember at the moment, at the Berlanga gate of this town, talking about some things that he cannot remember, this witness saw and heard how Gonzalo de Vargas said that his father lived to a good age ['a good hundred at least'], whom this witness knew had died a Jew, and this witness and those present told him not to say that, and that his father had sinned in dying a Jew. Gonzalo de Vargas said that his father having died a Jew was no sin, because he had died in his Law as a Jew.

(d) The roles reversed: statement by Francisco de Torres

[From *Fontes*, iv, p. 526n]

If the king our lord should order the Christians to become Jews and [rather] they left his kingdoms, some would become Jews and others would leave, and those who left, once they saw that they were lost, would have to become Jews in order to return to their nature [*naturaleza*]. And they would be Christians and would pray like Christians and would deceive the world. [People] would say that they were Jews and inside, in the heart and will, they would be Christians.

18. Massacre of New Christians in Lisbon

Conversion to Christianity did not solve the problems of Jews in Portugal any more than it had in Spain. In 1506, the massacres of 'New Christians' in the neighbouring country were repeated in what seems to have been a particularly violent form.

[From Damião de Gois, *Cronica de Don Manuel*, ed. Rodrigues Lapa, in *Historiadores quinhentistas*, Lisbon, 1972, pp. 110-14; in Portuguese]

In the monastery of St Dominic in [Lisbon], there is a chapel named after Jesus and in it a crucifix, in which at that time a sign was seen, to which they gave the colour of a miracle, although those who were to be found in the church judged to the contrary. Among the [sceptics], a New Christian said that a lighted candle appeared to him, which was placed beside the image of Jesus, and that some men from the lower orders who were there hauled him out of the church by his hair and killed him and immediately burned his body in the Ressio [a quarter of Lisbon].

To this disturbance many people came, to whom a friar gave a sermon, calling them together against the New Christians. After this two friars came out of the monastery with a crucifix in their hands, shouting, 'Heresy! heresy!'. This made such an impression on many foreigners, [who were] ordinary people, sailors from ships which had come at that time from Holland, Zeeland, Hoesteland [probably the Baltic] and other places, as well as men of the land [Portuguese], of the same [social] condition and low quality, that, more than five hundred having assembled, they began to kill all the New Christians they found in the streets. They threw the dead and dying bodies onto, and burnt them on, a bonfire which they had made in the Ribeira [the bank of the Tagus in Lisbon] and the Ressio. In this business they were helped by slaves and serving-lads, who with great diligence carted wood and other materials to light the fire. On this Easter Sunday they killed more than five hundred people.

This crowd of wicked men and friars, who, without fear of God, walked through the streets inciting the people to so great a cruelty, was joined by a thousand peasants, of the same kind as the others, and on [Easter] Monday they continued their wickedness together with greater cruelty. And seeing that by now they could not find any [more] New Christians in the streets, they attacked with battering-rams and ladders the houses in which they knew [the converts] were. They hauled them out, and, dragging them through the streets with their sons, wives and daughters, they threw them indiscriminately, dead and alive, onto the bonfires, without any mercy. And so great was the cruelty that they even executed children and babies in the cradle, taking them by the legs, cutting them into pieces and smashing them against walls. In these cruelties, they did not forget to sack the houses and steal all the gold, silver and jewels which they found in them, the matter reaching such a frenzy that they dragged [even] from the churches many men, women, boys and girls, tearing them away from the tabernacles [containing the Eucharistic bread] and from the images of Our Lord and **Our Lady** and the other **saints**, which they had embraced for fear of death, killing and burning without distinction, [and] without fear of God, both women and men.

On this day more than a thousand souls perished, without there being anyone in the city who dared resist, because of the small number of people of quality who were in it, those of highest rank being away because of the plague. If the magistrates and other justices showed an intention to attend to so great an evil they met so much resistance that they were forced to retreat where they could be sure that what had happened to the New Christians would not happen to them.

Among the Portuguese who occupied themselves with this business, which was so ugly and inhuman, there were some who, to avenge themselves for the hatred and illwill that they had for certain 'pure' Christians, gave the foreigners to understand that the New Christians were their enemies, and, in the streets or in their houses, wherever they came across them, they killed them, without anyone being able to impose order on such a disaster.

Once this day had gone by, which was the second of this persecution, on [Easter] Tuesday these damned men went back to pursue their cruelty, but not as much as on the other days, because by now they could not find anyone to kill, since all the New Christians who escaped this great fury were placed in safety by honourable and merciful people, who did whatever they could; and the time and its disorder permitted them, without being able to avoid the deaths in this tumult of more than nineteen hundred souls, who by all accounts were killed by these wicked and perverse men in the events of much of that day. In the afternoon of that same day, a senior councillor, Aires de Silva, and the governor [of Lisbon], Dom Alvaro de Castro, came to the city with those of their forces whom they could assemble, the fury of [the rioters] being by now almost exhausted and at peace, as they were tired of killing and without hope of being able to carry out any more robberies than they had already done.

This news reached the king in the town of Avis, where he was on the way from Abrantes to visit his mother Princess Beatriz, who was in Beja. He was very sad and angry about it, and so, to find out the truth about so great a disorder, he immediately sent from there the prior of the Crato and Dom Diogo Lobo, baron of Alvito, with powers to punish those who were found guilty, of whom many were imprisoned and hanged for justice, mainly among the [Portuguese] natives, because the foreigners returned to their ships with the stolen goods and spoils that they could carry, and each went back to his own hometown. The friars who [had] paraded through the city with the crucifix were defrocked and, after being sentenced, were burnt. And the king ordered proceedings through his official representative against [the people] in the city [of Lisbon] and its territory, as well as its officials, as a result of which many lost their offices and property, and sentence was given against the city and its territory.

19. The voice of the converso

As had happened previously in Spain, Portuguese converts from Judaism to Christianity sometimes expressed their unhappiness and confusion in poetic form.

[From Elvira Cunha de Azevedo Mea, *Orações judaicas na Inquisição Portuguesa – seculo XVI*, in *Jews and Conversos. Studies in society and the Inquisition*, ed. Yosef Kaplan, Jerusalem 1985, pp. 173-4; in Portuguese]

(a) On the Book of Judith

[Verses by Antônio Vaz, physician, Coimbra, 1583]

We know that we will not be defeated
By the force of powerful men,
Even if giants fight for them.

Only a weak woman went to fight,
Judith, the daughter of Adalanith.
Apart from her looks
She carried within her breast
[the intention] to kill **Holofernes**
and not to return to her people
but rather die.
She dressed in clothes to please,
Abandoning her widow's weeds,
She put perfume on her face and hands.
She so captivated him
that she cut off his head with a third blow.

The people were astonished
to see such great daring
and such great valour
in a woman.
The least [of people] began to
kill the strongest,
the weak destroyed the powerful.
Because you, Lord, followed them
and heard their prayer with favour,

We praise the Lord
and give you new praise for these mercies.
You alone are a great Lord,
great is your virtue.
Salvation will not fail the one who
calls upon you.

(b) A Song for Passover

[From Amílcar Paulo, 'O ritual dos criptojudeus portugueses (algumas reflexões sobre os seus ritos), in Yosef Kaplan, ed., *Jews and conversos*, pp. 146-7; in Portuguese]

Adonai is a Hebrew title for God; *Senhor meu* is Portuguese for 'my lord'.

Adonai, adonai, adonai, senhor meu
Let us sing today to the Lord,
God of singular glory,
Who threw the horse and the rider to the bottom of the sea.
As a conquering hero may his Name be 'the Omnipotent'.
He consumed the chariot and army of Pharaoh.
Famous generals and valiant soldiers also
Were buried with him in the Red Sea....
Your great arm, Lord, a magnificent fortress,
Strong against the harsh enemy,
Defeating him with ferocity, you put down your foes,
Prostrate at so much glory,
Who will, by your anger, be cut down like weak straw.
The flowing wave appeared, strong winds were not lacking,
And in the midst of an abyss, the waters gathered together.
Let us go on our way and walk.
We shall praise the God of Israel, who delivered us from Egypt,
From that king so cruel.
Our Law is holy, worthy of all praise.
All will say with me, Blessed be the Lord.
Israelites, join together with the people of Moses,
Who have the holy Law from God,
It is with the **Hebrew** people.

20. The Rabbis on conversion

The conversion of large numbers of people from Judaism to Christianity inevitably raised the question of motives. After the departure of thousands of Jews from Spain, as a result of the expulsion edict of 1492, the issue became one of religious identity.

[From: Moisés Orfali Levi, *Los conversos españoles en la literatura rabínica. Problemas jurídicos y opiniones legales durante los siglos XII-XVI*, Salamanca, 1982, pp. 32-3, 41-2; in Spanish translation from Hebrew]

(a) Before the 1492 expulsion: Rabbi Shamah ben Shlomo Durán (Algeria, c. 1450)

We even presume to say that not only forced converts but also forced apostates, even in the case of incest, continue to be part of Israel. Their marriages are marriages; their act of repudiation [divorce] an act of repudiation; their **levirate** is a levirate, their legal rites are legal. Not only theirs but also those of their children born in apostasy: Israel, even when uncircumcised [physically], is circumcised *mahul* [spiritually].

Rabbi Simón ben Shlomo Durán (Lived from 1439 to about 1510)

It is more than ninety years since in Christian lands, because of anti-Jewish persecutions and decrees, many men, women and children were converted. This generation of converts, although they were able to flee to nearby **Ishmaelite** lands to return to their old faith, did not do so, but rather remained among the [Christian] Gentiles and had sons and daughters there. The same happened with their children, until their descendants, belonging to the third and fourth generation[s], felt the urge to return to the God of Israel. They fled, therefore, from **Edomite** lands to lands of Ishmael, where they returned to their former religion. During their stay in gentile lands, the majority of these converts contracted marriage with other converts. Only a minority contracted marriage with the children of Edom ['old' Christians]. Well then, one of them, of the third or fourth generation, came here and converted and, having converted, married and died without descendants. Now I ask: is the widow free of levirate or not? It turns out that a *converso* brother of the husband is living in gentile lands, both he and his father having been born there. The answer is 'Yes' [she is exempt].

(b) After the 1492 expulsion: Rabbi Shmuel de Medina (Salonika, Greece, 1506-1589)

Every *converso* who had the opportunity to abandon Spain or Portugal to return to Judaism and did not do so is [nonetheless] considered a Jew.

This applies to inheritance but not in the case of levirate.... [Such a person] is disinherited because he had many years in which to return [to Judaism] but did not return, whereby he lost the right to inherit.... As far as levirate is concerned we confirm that forced converts are part of Israel....

With respect to what I said before about one who is forced to convert, that although he has sinned, he is an Israelite,... it is appropriate to examine the situation of those converts who survived the persecution and remained there for many years among the gentiles, their persecutors, without abandoning that place and going to another country, where they might serve God openly and without fear. If there are any among them who had the opportunity to emigrate and did not take advantage of it, but rather, being forced at the beginning, afterwards moved away from Torah and [now] voluntarily practise Gentile customs, these, and those like them, have no part with the God of Israel and it is unnecessary to add that their testimony is not valid [in Jewish courts], since they are lower than the Gentiles.

Rabbi Binyamin Ze'ev ben Matitiahu (Greece, mainly Arta, late fifteenth- to mid-sixteenth centuries)

I was consulted when some of our people arrived in the holy community of Arta from the captivity of Apulia [in southern Italy]. Among them there arrived a woman called Floba, who had been married there to an apostate from the whole Torah, because of the Christian religion: [she attended] churches and [observed Christian] precepts and customs, to such a point that, living there, she forgot the religion of Israel, and had lived with [this converso] for a long time in this state of perversion.

But when the king of Spain's edict came out forbidding to remain in their territories not only any Jew but also any apostate [i.e. converso], all these communities left, with their Judaism, their faith and their prayer [lit. 'sanctification of the Name (of God)'], and they arrived in these other lands of our lord, His Royal Highness. There also came with them men, women and children from among those who were apostates, and among them the aforesaid woman called Floba, with whom we are concerned here.

That accursed man, who had confined her in his house in submission to the Christian religion, did not wish to return either to his people or to his God. Further, he bribed some people in the Court to allow him to remain, when some faithful Jews gave testimony against him.

In any case, when this woman decided to go back to the service of the Name of the Lord her God, she wanted to take a husband according to the Law of Moses and of Israel, but there rose against her false men from among those who 'do not see the light' [Job 3:16: 'Or put away like a still-born child that never came to be, like unborn babes that never see the light'], who said to her: 'How are you going to marry this man, if you were married there to that other one? Until you receive the act of repudiation from him, you remain united with him'. But she argues thus: 'He never married me according to the Law of Moses and of Israel, but rather he married me before those people's bishop, and with invalid witnesses'.

Therefore, she does not need him to give her the act of repudiation.

Other European expulsions

21. Bohemia, 1427

Letter from Pope Martin V to the provost of Mount Saint Peter, Brno, 1 February 1427

[From Simonsohn, no. 643, p. 749; in Latin]

Martin [etc.] to our beloved son the provost of the church of Mount St Peter in Brno, in the **diocese** of Olmutz, greeting…. Previously distracted by various causes, we hereby very much desire that, in churches and particular places the Most High [the **Blessed Sacrament**] should be venerated with devotion and careful study Also that, with the intention of doing reverence to the Supreme Majesty, the divine cult should everywhere be observed. Since, on the part of our beloved sons, the magistrates, councillors and **commune** of the town of Yglavia [*sic*] in the diocese of Olmutz, a petition recently shown to us contained [the information] that, since for other reasons our beloved son and nobleman Albert, duke of Austria and of the **March** of Moravia, to whose temporal jurisdiction this same town is subject, considering it prudent that since the Jews, who had their homes in the said town and also a synagogue in it, were causing trouble among the Christian faithful, he should expel the Jews from the said town [did so], and in the same way ordered their houses to be distributed among these same Christian faithful, assigning them to [Christians]. In this way, this community of [Jewish] inhabitants and residents [were expelled] from the kingdom of Bohemia, where, with many [other] perfidious enemies of the Christian name, and implicated in the errors of heretics [the **Hussites**], they might [otherwise] detestably cause new and serious injuries and dangers to souls….

[As in earlier centuries, the Jews were here suffering by association with dissident movements in the Church.]

22. Italy, 1504

The expulsion of the Jews from Piacenza in 1504

[From Simonsohn, *The Jews of the duchy of Milan*, 2, pp. 962-3; in Italian]

Summoned ... in the aforesaid place ... by command [the names of the city councillors follow].

The royal letter [of the occupying French ruler Louis XII], dated in Milan on 8 February 1504, having first been read, together with the petition of the Magnificent Commune of Piacenza, against the Jews who were to be freed [*sic*] from this our city, the aforesaid elders [*Anziani*] urgently requested the aforesaid lord magistrate [*podestà*] to put this letter into effect as it stands. The lord *podestà* declared that he was ready to comply with and put into practice everything and every particular that fell to him, as set out in the letter, and ordered the Jews who were living in that city at the time to be brought to him. In the presence of Lazaro son of Calman and Lazaro son of another Lazaro, deceased, both Jews, who listened and understood, he told them to their faces that they should leave that city in the next three days and leave the territory of Piacenza, on pain of two hundred gold **ducats**, in cash, to be allocated, half to the [French] king's chamber and the other half to the aforesaid Commune of Piacenza; and, in addition, so that no-one at any time may pretend ignorance, he revoked, and does revoke, his own proclamations or those made in his name in recent days, that no-one must harm those Jews, and in addition he ordered that, at the end of the next three days, it should be announced publicly in that city, at the sound of the trumpet, in the accustomed places, that the aforesaid proclamation [of protection] has been revoked and is of no value.

Moreover the said lord Prior and elders ... unanimously provided and ordained that no Jews should, at any time in the future, be introduced or admitted to live in the said city of Piacenza, or in its diocese; and that, if anyone dares to speak of, or secure the reception of such Jews, they intended and intend that anyone who works to the advantage of the Jews in this way will incur a fine of fifty gold ducats,... to be applied half to the royal chamber and the other half to the aforesaid Commune of Piacenza; since the minds of these presiding lords is firm and established that these Jews, and the rest of the Jewish people, who are both strong enemies of the Christian faith and of the citizens [of Piacenza], and depopulators of cities and peoples, should not at any time in the future be allowed to live or act in this same city; wishing and intending that, under the aforesaid penalties, any agents or supporters of this depraved generation [of Jews] should be had and held and reputed as rebels and enemies of their native land, and of the Republic of Piacenza and of the Christian faith, and should be deprived, as by this present [order] they are deprived, of all privileges, honours, dignities and **immunities** which they enjoyed in each and every thing which belongs to the city and diocese of Piacenza.

III: Jews in the European economy

There are two main aspects of the involvement of Jews in the European economy of the late medieval and early modern periods which have to be considered here. In all western European countries with Jewish populations in this period, there were restrictions on the economic roles which Jews might fulfil. These were justified on theological as much as economic grounds, and are represented in the Church policies referred to in chapter I above. In the great majority of cases, the result of these policies was to confine Jews to trade and finance, whatever their personal inclinations may have been. Although examples are given of Jews who performed various economic functions in this period, in public or private capacities, the chapter begins with a contemporary account of how Jews were commonly perceived by the Christian majority. Bernáldez's reflection of views which prevailed not only in Spain but all over Western and Central Europe at the time, is followed by two pieces of legislation, also from Spain, which indicate at least the theoretical role of Jews in the last years of the Castilian community. The first of these is a section from the laws which were issued in Valladolid in 1412 by the government of John II of Castile, while the second, dating from twenty years later and also issued in Valladolid, originated in the Jewish community itself. Even in translation, the differing styles of the earlier and later documents reflect their respective Castilian and Hebrew origins. It should be noted that the 1412 laws applied to Muslims (referred to as 'Moors' in the text) as well as Jews, while the 1432 legislation applied to Jews alone.

The effectiveness or otherwise of such legislation (which had its parallels in the other countries of Jewish settlement in Western and Central Europe in this period), is considered in the succeeding documents. Thus, despite the 1412 prohibition of royal tax collection by Jews, as late as 1488, just four years before the Spanish expulsion edict, a Jew might still obtain a national contract to collect taxes for the Castilian Crown.* The succeeding texts, culled from the rich archival sources of Spain and Italy, which surpass those of other areas in the period, show fifteenth-century Jews as moneylenders, lawyers, physicians, and even, in Castile, as royal treasurers. The 1472 mandate to a tax-collector in the Papal states gives a detailed picture of the diffusion of Jewish settlement in the area, as well as the varied levels of economic prosperity which might be achieved by Jews in that period.

* See document 28 below, p. 81.

23. The Jewish stereotype: Spain, 1492

A chronicler's comments after the 1492 expulsion.

[From Andres Bernáldez, *Memorias*, pp. 97-8; in Spanish]

They did not believe in giving reward to God by means of virginity and chastity: all their effort was to grow and multiply. And during the time of the rise of this heretical depravity by *converso* gentlemen and merchants [in Seville], many monasteries were violated and and many professed nuns corrupted and subjected to ridicule, some by bribes and some by deceptions, [these converts] not believing in or fearing excommunication. Rather, they did it all to injure Jesus Christ and the Church. And in general, for the most part, they were a profiteering people, with many arts and deceits, because they all lived from idle jobs and they had no conscience when buying or selling with Christians. They never wanted to take jobs such as ploughing or digging, or walking through the fields looking after flocks, nor did they teach such things to their children, but rather [they took] jobs in the town, and sitting down making their living with little effort. In these kingdoms, many of them gained great wealth and property in a short time, because they had no conscience about profit and usury, saying that they gained everything from their enemies, clinging to the saying that God ordered the people of Israel, in their departure to Israel, to rob Egypt by art and deceit, demanding from them as loans their vases and gold and silver cups.

24. Economic laws: Spain, 1412, 1432

(a) Legislation by the Castilian government for the regulation of Jewish and Muslim life in the kingdom: the 'Valladolid Laws' of John II of Castile, 2 January 1412.

[From Baer, *Die Juden*, 2, pp. 265-6; in Spanish]

(2) Also that no Jew or Moor should be a spice-seller or pharmacist or surgeon or medical doctor. Nor should they sell bread or wine or flour or [olive] oil or animal fat [*manteca*], or anything else edible, to Christian men and women, nor should they have shops or stores or stalls, whether public or hidden, to sell any kind of edible food. And any Jew who does anything to the contrary should incur a penalty of 2,000 *maravedis* for each offence, and, in addition, their bodies should be at my mercy, so that they may be ordered to receive corporal punishment, as has been thoroughly examined and belongs to my mercy.

(5) Also that no Jews or Moors should be tax-farmers or legal representatives [*procuradores*] or collectors of customs dues [*almojarifes*], or stewards or collectors of my [royal] rents or for any other Christian lord or lady, or among themselves. Nor should they practise these offices, or any one of them, nor should they be **brokers** ... or moneychangers, nor should the said Jews or Moors, or any one of them, carry any weapons in cities, towns or villages. And any Jew ... or Moor ... who goes against this, or against any part of it, should pay as a penalty for each offence 2,000 *maravedis*, and Christians, of whatever estate they may be, who employ a Jew ... or Moor ... to exercise such offices, or any one of them, should pay that same fine for each offence.

(6) Also that none or any of the said Jews and Moors should have, in their quarters or areas or dwellings, squares or markets [in which] to sell or buy anything for Christians to eat or drink, on pain of [a fine of] five hundred *maravedis* from each of them for each offence, but that they may have and sell, and should have and sell, such things for themselves, in the areas where they live.

(b) The Takkanot [Laws] of Valladolid, 1432, which were produced by the Jewish communities themselves, under the authority of the Castilian government. The whole of the first paragraph is a series of reasons justifying the action ordered in the second paragraph. 'Denunciations' refers to the practice whereby persons were relieved of communal taxes when they reported certain crimes or misdemeanours.

[From *De iure hispano-hebraico. Las taqqanot de Valladolid de 1432. Un estatuto comunal renovador*, ed. and trans. Yolanda Moreno Koch, *Fontes Iudæorum Regni Castellae*, v, Salamanca, 1987, pp. 71-3; in Spanish translation from Hebrew]

Chapter 4. Concerning taxes and [feudal] services.

Seeing that, for our sins, taxpayers, who by law are obliged to pay, free themselves of the obligation, and distribute [the sum demanded] so that other Jews pay it. Also, some of the Jews dwelling in the said kingdom of Castile, by means of their denunciations, act so as to remove and take away from the communities [*kehillot*], may their **Rock** and Saviour keep them, where they live, the taxes of the said lord king (may God guard him) and act, concerning the [feudal] **aids** [*servicios*] for which they are obliged, so as to remove from them the taxes for which they are obliged: and others go to certain places which are under **seigneurial jurisdiction**, [to obtain] certain **liberties** that are given, and ordered to be given and announced, so that they may be free from the taxes of the said lord king, God keep him. Whereby the royal towns are depopulated, both the places which contribute to aids and others, which is a disservice to the said lord king, and from it comes great harm to the [Jewish] communities, may their Rock and Saviour guard them. And certain others obtain letters of favour [*cartas de merced*] from the said lord king, whom God preserve, and confirmations of certain privileges which they possess, and others send in people to ask or threaten, [so that] they stop paying or [else] pay what they like, or so that the [Jewish] communities, may their Rock and Saviour preserve them, make a contract with them where they live; and, in times past, their ancestors, may they rest in paradise, in their laws [*takkanot*] in Castile, made laws about this.

Therefore we order that no Jew, male or female, should obtain a letter from the said lord king, may God preserve him, nor from the said queen our lady, blessed may she be among women, nor from any other lord or lady or prince or powerful person, allowing any kind of exemption from what they are obliged to pay in tax, or may be or is allocated [to them] in the taxes of the communities [*kehillot*], may their Rock and Saviour preserve them, nor obtain confirmation of any privilege concerning this, nor set a petitioner or threatener [*sic*] against any person outside the terms of our Law, nor profit from any order or request which may come from their part, nor receive it, either for him or herself for any community, or for any other person or persons, nor should any community benefit from any release or grant which may come to them in this way, so that they should not pay the taxes assigned to them, both in aids [*servicios*] and in **requests** [*pedidos*] or forced loans [*emprestidos*], or in any *maravedis* at all that the said lord king, whom God preserve, may demand from the communities, may their Rock and Saviour preserve them.

25. The Jew as royal tax-farmer: Spain, 1488

Yuçef Abravanel is appointed *recaudador mayor* [chief collector] of the royal taxes on livestock [*servicio y montazgo de los ganados*].

[From Suárez Fernández, *Documentos*, pp. 311-12, dated 30 November 1488; in Spanish]

Don Ferdinand and Dona Isabella [etc.]. We make it known to you, our chief accountants [*contadores mayores*] that, in recognition and consideration of the many good, loyal and agreeable services that Don Yuçef Abravanel has done for us and continues to do each day, and as some amends, satisfaction and remuneration for them, it is our grace

and will to do him favour, and by this present we enact that he should
be our chief collector of the taxes of *servicio* and *montazgo* of livestock
for these our kingdoms and lordships, which same collectorship we
wish that the said Don Yuçef Abravanel should have and hold, and one
heir whom he may name and have, for all the days of their lives, that
is of each of them, with thirty *maravedis* and other things for which the
said rent of the *servicio* and *montazgo* was farmed this year, which
began on the day of Saint John [the Baptist] in June [24th], and
which will be completed on the day of St John in June in the first year
coming from our Lord, of 1489 years, and from then on what it may
be worth for all the days of the lives of the said Don Yuçef Abravanel
and the said heir whom he may name and possess.

26. The Jew as moneylender: Italy, 1479; Spain, 1480

(a) Duchy of Milan, 1479

[From Simonsohn, *Jews in the duchy of Milan*, vol. 12, pp. 778-9; in Latin]

Given at Milan on 3 April 1479

The dukes of Milan [etc.].... The spokesmen [*oratores*] of the
venerable provost of our territory of Pizzighettone, and Antonio Lissa
of the commune of the said territory, have been before us, as well as
Calamano, a Jew and inhabitant of that same land: and the above
spokesmen urged that, in order to avoid ecclesiastical censures, the
said Calamano wished to renounce certain things concerning which
undertakings [*capituli*] with him had been entered into by that same
commune. Calamano himself is at one with the aforesaid men. He
stated and promised that he wished to renounce these said agreements
[and respond] to every request of these aforesaid men. Since, however,
this same Calamano doubts whether he may not be required at some
time [in the future], through the malice of individuals, to be removed
and expelled from the said land, he asked if any other Jew would be
judged sufficient in his place. Since he affirmed that he would thus be
greatly inconvenienced, if he did these things, we should take counsel
at once and give dispensation, so that he might be able to live in the
said land and carry on his business. We therefore, judging their
petition not to be dishonest [*ab honestate non aliena*], given that our
Holy Mother Church tolerates Jews living in all its lands, by these our
letters acknowledge it to be proper that the said Calamano should
renounce these said agreements. We concede and grant dispensation
so that he may be allowed to live in the said land of Pizighettone and

carry on his business, and we give order to the commissioner and commune of Pizzighettone that, during the time of the abandonment of the said agreements, they should not expel the said Calamano or admit any other Jew into the said land, or allow any undue interference or novelty against him and his family or against their goods.

(b) Action is demanded by the Crown against the Jews of Avila, in a letter from Medina del Campo, on 18 December 1480

[From Suárez Fernández, *Documentos*, pp. 194–5; in Spanish]

Don Ferdinand and Doña Isabella [etc.] … to you, the community [*aljama*] of the Jews of the city of Avila, and to each one of you, salutation and grace. Know that it has been reported to us, in a petition from the good men [*'omes buenos'*] and the councils of the district [*sexmo*, lit. 'sixth'] of Santiago [Saint James] in the territory and jurisdiction of the said city, that they undertook a certain legal process against you concerning usury [*los logros*] before Dr Pedro Sánchez de Frías of our [Royal] Council and our *corregidor* of that city, in which he gave a sentence which was appealed against by the said councils and the good men of the said district. And they had sent the record of this appeal to be presented in our Council, and the said appeal was refused to them. And in accordance with the said appeal, or in the best form that they could, and which was required by law, they had it sent to be presented before us in our Council, and they said that the aforementioned sentence and everything done by the said judge was null and void, and declared their grievance against the said judge, who did not see fit to grant the said appeal, and against Juan de Arévalo, public scribe in the said city, who refused to give them [the records of] the case. And they asked of us a favour, that we should provide for them in this matter with justice, ordering that our letter of summons should be given to them against you about this, and [one] of restraint, so that while the said case is pending you should not carry out any act or move in this matter until the said process has been examined in our Council and justice has been done concerning it. And to the said scribe, that he should hand over the said process at once, in the due form.

And because you ought to be summoned and heard concerning [this matter], we order this letter to be issued in that meaning, whereby we command you that, with your aforesaid community having assembled, as is your use and custom, if this can be achieved, or, if not, with the knowledge of three or four of the principal Jews in that city, from the day on which this letter is notified to you in the above form, [after

twenty days] you should appear in our High Court [*audiencia*] before
our judges [*oidores*], in accordance with the above, to speak and allege
from your Law whatever you wish to say and allege concerning this
and to conclude and complete the arguments, and to hear a sentence
or sentences, including even the definitive sentence and allocation of
costs, and the other acts at which by [Castilian] law you should be
present and specially called, by this present we summon and cite you.
And if it should appear that we must order you to listen to and keep
your [own] Law, or else if you are rebellious, we shall order justice to
be done in the matter without summoning you or awaiting you
further. And we order the scribe before whom passed the process
concerning the above to hand it over at once to the legal representatives of the said *sexmo* of Santiago in due form, closed and sealed,
paying him his just salary which he ought to have for this....

27. The Jew as lawyer: Spain, 1484

The *corregidor* of Trujillo is told by the Crown not to allow a Jewish lawyer
to continue practising.

[From Suárez Fernández, *Documentos*, pp. 240-1, given at Córdoba, 24
September 1484; in Spanish]

Don Ferdinand and Doña Isabella [etc.], to you, Licentiate Lope
Sánchez del Castillo, our *corregidor* in the town of Trujillo, salutation
and grace. Know that we have been told that although we have
forbidden and banned Don Mayr, a Jew, citizen of this town, to
practise the office of advocate or lawyer [*letrado*] under certain
disabilities, in accordance with the laws of our kingdoms which forbid
and ban such a thing, because at the time when this order and ban was
issued against him, the queen was in that town and the said Don Mayr
stopped practising, but since then, disregarding the penalties which
were established there and what was commanded by us, he has
resumed the practice of the said office of advocacy and is [now]
practising it, and the town gives him a salary for it, and he goes into
council meetings in the said town, which is against the laws of our
kingdoms. And that the aforesaid Jew, so that the documents and
memoranda that he produces should not appear to be his, does not sign
them. And yet the town's magistrates admit them, and because of this
many people suffer great fraud and detriment in their processes and
cases. As a result, appeal was made to us, that we should provide in this
[matter] as we may understand to be in compliance with our service,
or as our will may be. And we found this good.

Therefore we order that, as soon as you have investigated the above, and if you find it to be thus, you should provide [in this matter] as you ought according to justice, and henceforth you should not allow or give occasion to the said Don Mayr to practise the said office of advocacy, or to enter the council meetings of that town, or collect any fee or salary for it. And that henceforth, in the documents and memoranda that we have presented before you, you should keep to the tenor and form of the law made by us in the **Cortes** of Toledo, which discusses this case. And neither you nor any other officials should accept the aforesaid documents, unless they are signed by an advocate who produces them in accordance with what the aforesaid law disposes.

28. The Jew as royal treasurer: Spain, 1488

Abraham Seneor is appointed by the Catholic Monarchs as treasurer of the *Santa Hermandad* (Holy Brotherhood), a royal agency for law and order in Castile.

[From Suárez Fernández, *Documentos*, pp. 297-9. Valencia, 18 March 1488: in Spanish]

Don Ferdinand and Doña Isabella [etc.].... For certain reasons which are to our service, recognising the good and loyal services that we have received from you, Don Abraham Seneor, citizen of the city of Segovia, and for your good diligence and fidelity, by this present we provide you to the office of the treasury-general of the Holy Brotherhood of all our kingdoms and lordships, so that you, or whoever has your authority, signed with your name and sealed by a public scribe and by no other person at all, may receive and collect all the *maravedis* from the [public] contribution to the said Brotherhood of our said kingdoms and lordships, from fifteen days into the coming April of the current year, after the issue of this letter. . .so that you should pay out of [these *maravedis*] the salary that the [*Hermandad*] people have and ought to have, who are paid and should be paid by the said Brotherhood, and all the other expenses and costs which we may order to be paid from the said fund. And that you should possess and levy this and have it paid to you with all the rights and salaries attached and belonging to the said office, in the same way as the former treasurers of the said Brotherhood levied them and were entitled to levy them, in such a way that you should not lack for anything as a result....

For, by this present, we provide the said office to you, the said Don
Abraham Seneor, and we command the reverend father in Christ, the
bishop of Palencia, our chief chaplain and confessor and our president
in the said *Hermandad*, and the vicar-general [*provisor*] of Villafranca
our chief sacristan, and Alfonso de Quintanilla, our chief accountant of
the said Brotherhood, and the **Licentiate** of Illescas, all in our [Royal]
Council, who are present in our name in the said Brotherhood, that as
soon as they see this our letter they should give and issue to you our
letter of [revenue] collection for all the provinces of our aforesaid
kingdoms and lordships, that you, and any persons you may name and
who may have your authorisation, may collect and receive all that is
owed in the said contribution to the said *Hermandad* in the said our
kingdoms and lordships, from the said fifteenth day of the month of
August coming, in so far as is our favour and will, so that you may
have and levy it, and have it paid to you, with all the said rights and
salaries attached and belonging to the said office of the said treasury,
just as was ordered to be paid and was paid to the said treasurers that
there have been up to now of the said *Hermandad*....

29. The Jew as physician: Italy, 1462,1474

(a) Pisa, 1462: an agreement made between a Jewish doctor and his Christian
patient in Pisa in 1462.

[From Michele Luzzati, 'Il medico ebreo e il contadino: un documento pisano
del 1462', in *La casa dell'Ebreo. Saggi sugli Ebrei a Pisa e in Toscana nel
Medioevo e nel Rinascimento*, Pisa, 1985, pp. 56-7; in Italian]

Master Bonomo, son of the late Samuel, Jew, doctor, on the one part,
and Agostino Olivi of the commune of Sant' Andrèa in Pescaiola on the
other, wishing to hold to and be effectively obliged by all and every
thing written below, have arrived at this pact and agreement, that is
to say that the said Master Bonomo should be obliged to and must heal
[or cure = *medere*] the aforesaid Agostino and deliver the same of the
infirmity which he has in his right knee-joint, which joint the aforesaid
Agostino cannot extend or stretch out, and this without iron and fire
and the breaking of bones [? *roctoro*], ... that is to say with hot
compresses [*stufiis*], ... and ointments, so that the same aforesaid
Agostino may extend the aforesaid knee and joint in the same way as
he can [use] his left knee, and so that he can walk well and uprightly,
and this in a time and period of less than six months. And that the
same Master Bonomo should be obliged to acquire with his own
money the medicines and ointments necessary for the aforesaid cure,

and that the said Agostino, if he is freed [of his condition] in the aforesaid interval of time, so that the aforesaid joint and knee can be extended and walked on uprightly, is held and obliged to give and release to the same Master Bonomo, for his labour and of his [Agostino's] mercy, twelve full gold ducats; and, if the aforesaid Agostino is not freed within the said interval of six months, that each one of them should be freed and absolved of the things contained in this present instrument [document].

(b) Florence, 1474: Pope Sixtus IV grants a licence to Moses Pess to treat Christian patients in Florence, provided that he ensures that his Christian patients receive the last rites of the Catholic Church before treatment.

[From Shlomo Simonsohn, *The Apostolic See and the Jews: Documents: 1464–1521*, Toronto, 1990, pp. 1216-17, document dated at Rome, 3 November 1474; in Latin]

Sixtus, bishop, servant of the servants of God. To Moses Pess, Hebrew, doctor and knight of Spain [*militi Ispano*], inhabitant of the city of Florence, [being] uncertain of the way of truth and with the intention that you may come to hold to what you do not [yet] know. Since you, and other Jews, whom the most holy Church tolerates in various parts of the world as a witness to Jesus Christ, and allows to remain in your great hardness of heart and blindness, rather than know [and understand] the secrets of the words of the prophets and of the holy scriptures, and come to the news and the grace of salvation in the Christian faith, because at length you appeal to us for our protection and favours, out of the gentleness of Christian piety, above all in those things for which Christians hope in the future, we have no wish to deny to you, so that, attracted by such mercy, you may recognize your errors and, enlightened by heavenly grace, you may manage to come at length to the true light of clarity, which is Christ. Indeed, the petition which has been displayed before us on your behalf said that you, who have long dedicated yourself to the work of medicine, and who are now a great master and expert in that [subject], also wish to be able to minister without penalty to believers in Christ who come to you in their infirmities, and to receive from you medicines to cure them, as you know how to proceed, according to the reason of the body [*phisice rationem*] and the canons of medicine.

We therefore, having been informed by reliable account of your excellence, knowledge and learning in the aforesaid art, being favourable to your supplications in this matter, of our special gift favour you, so that all Christian believers should obtain medicine for their infirmities from you, and so that you may receive medicines with which to cure them, and that you may administer medicines and healthy antidotes to these same Christians, according to the reason of physic and medicine, every time it happens that you are called out to these same sick Christians, [order] that before you minister to these same Christian believers, they should receive the sacraments of the Church, and [thus] receive spiritual medicine for themselves and for the salvation of their souls, according to the statutes of the general [Fourth Lateran] council. [In this way] you may freely and licitly provide [such services], when alerted and requested, and not any other matters or any other kind [of medicine], notwithstanding any other provisions to the contrary

30. Papal taxation of Jews: Italy, 1472

A commission and mandate to Jacopo di Aquasparta, to collect the tax of the **twentieth** [*vigesima*] from Jews in the provinces of Campania and Maritima.

[From Simonsohn, *Documents: 1464-1521*, pp. 1197-200. Dated at Rome, 25 June 1472; in Latin]

To our beloved son Jacopo di Aquasparta, greetings in the Lord.

Seeing that your faithfulness, sincerity and diligence and experience in getting things done have been proved in many matters, we have thus been persuaded to commit and trust the business of the Apostolic Chamber to you. Since, then, the twentieth, imposed by our most holy lord the pope for the needs of the Catholic faith, has to be demanded from all the Jews living throughout the provinces, cities, territories and villages which are indirectly or directly subject to the Holy Roman Church, and, because of the distance of the provinces, it is necessary to depute various agents to carry out this business, we, having, in the Lord, complete trust in your abovementioned faithfulness and diligence, ... commit to you and order you that, going to the provinces of Campagna and Maritima, and every single place within them where Jews live, according to the list given below, should demand and raise the sums set out below for the aforesaid twentieth, as instructed. We give you full and free faculty and power to summon those Jews, each and every one of them, to you, with the effect of employing all ways and means which may occur to you to coerce and compel them. Also, we order each and every official in the aforesaid provinces and places here named, that, if they should be summoned before you to carry out the abovementioned business, they should grant you all possible favours, if they wish to retain our most holy lord the pope's favour and our own....

[There follows a list of places with Jewish inhabitants, giving some names, details of the number of households in each place, and the amounts to be paid, in ducats.]

	Ducats
Velletri: four houses	12
Sermoneta	
Master Angelo, doctor	60
Master Manuele	30
Leone de Cresci	20
Abraham	3
Sezze	
Mosce [Moses] de Mosecto	60
Mosce de Angelo	30
Terracina: six houses	
Cresci	20
Begnamine	20
Dattilo	3
Iacobbe	3
Moyse	3
[His] children	3
Piperno: seven houses	
Angelo de Mele	60
Bonaventura	25
Bonaventura	16
The other four houses	12
Castro - Salomone	5
Fresolone - Moscie	3
Alatro - Ventura	
Eliuccio	3
Two widowed women	3
Veroli: four houses	12
Fiorentino	
Mele and his brother	70
The heir of Salomone	20
Consiglio de Gagio	3
Abraham	3
Salomone	3

Pontecorvo: Vitale   25
    Salomone   20
    Diotaiuti and Mele   6
    Mosce   3

Anagni
    Aliuccio de Vitale   30
    Abraham de Sabbatuccio   20
    Master Angelo Hebreo [the Jew]   6
    Elia   4
    Manuele   3

Segne: three houses
    Abraham   8
    The other two   6

Patrica
    David and his brother   10
    Elia   10

Pelestrina: four houses
    Sabbatuccio   10
    The other three houses   9

Paliano: two houses   6

Genezano: four houses
    Menunzolo   4
    The other three houses   9

Cavi: three houses
    Elia   8
    Sabbatuccio   6
    The other house   3

Collepardo: one house   5

Maenza: one house   2

Piglio: one house   3

Vallemontone: seven houses
    Master Salomone   50
    The other six houses   18

Tibuli: fourteen houses   42

Subbiaco: one house   30

[The above list was sealed and dated at Rome on 25 June 1472.]

IV: Jews in European society

In various respects, the division of material between this chapter and the previous one is somewhat arbitrary, as it is hardly possible to make an effective separation between social and economic matters. Nonetheless, whereas chapter III is primarily concerned with Jewish economic activities for their own sake, and Jews' financial relations with Christian rulers, this chapter concentrates on other aspects of the dealings which went on between European Jews and their Christian neighbours. As in chapter III, extracts are included from Castilian laws of 1412 and 1432, which even though they are legal prescriptions, give a vivid picture of day-to-day relations between Jews and Christians, in Spain and elsewhere. They go well beyond the general injunctions of the Church, and also demonstrate the importance of clothes, jobs and sexual activity in determining the nature and extent of relations between the two communities. However, as in the 'economic' documents included earlier, the Castilian records of the last years of legal Jewish existence in the kingdom indicate that practice fairly rarely corresponded to theory. Thus it was still necessary, in 1491, for Ferdinand and Isabella's government to try to enforce the wearing of badges by Jews. A Castilian document of 1482 indicates that Jews were subject to violence on the roads, even before the build-up to the expulsion.

While the programme of the Fourth Lateran Council continued to be implemented, with varying degrees of efficiency and commitment, in Spain as in other countries, Italy was still able to produce vivid indications of the real nature of Jewish-Christian relations in the period. Thus, before accounts of social separation involving Jews in Spain and Italy, including even starvation tactics in the case of Spain, a document is presented in which Jews and Christians appear to have been involved in a kidnapping in Perugia Meanwhile in Castile, and later in the rest of Spain, the opinion grew in certain circles that baptism could never turn a Jew into a Christian. The first known example of the public proclamation of such a view took place in Toledo in 1449, and the vital section of the relevant text is included here. Later, such notions transferred themselves to Portugal, though, as an early sixteenth-century example indicates, it was still possible there, as in Spain in the same period, to buy or, as in this case, receive exemption from the penalties attached to Jewish, as to Muslim or heretical Christian ancestry.

The last, fairly lengthy, section of this chapter concerns a false accusation against Jews which went back to twelfth-century England. This was the charge that Jews habitually, and from time to time, kidnapped Christian children (almost always boys) and subjected them to torments which were intended to repeat those supposedly suffered by Christ at Jewish hands. * *Two such cases are referred to in the documents. The first is an Italian example, which involved the death of an Italian child called Simon, in Trent in 1475, while the second, which is described here at greater length, concerns the so called 'Holy Child' of La Guardia, who supposedly died in 1490. Although the pope tried to put an end to the Italian case, it is clear that no such effort was made to prevent the deaths, in Spain, of several Jews and Jewish converts to Christianity, who were accused of murdering a child who was never reported lost and whose body was never found, but whose supposed guilt greatly assisted the Inquisition in its campaign to secure the expulsion of Spain's Jews by the Catholic Monarchs, Ferdinand and Isabella. Some of the remaining trial documents are translated here, as well as an elaborate account of the resulting myth, published in 1533 by Sebastián de Horozco.*

31. Social laws in Spain: 1412, 1432

(a) Laws of Valladolid, 1412

[From: Baer, *Die Juden*, 2, pp. 266-9: in Spanish]

(4) Also that no male or female Jew or Moor, whether inside their houses or outside them, shall eat or drink among Christians ... or Christians ... among Jews ... or Moors.... Also that Jews ... or Moors ... should not have Christian squires or household servants, serving lads or lasses, to do them service or [be at] their command, or do any domestic task in their houses or cook food for them or do any domestic task for them on the Sabbath day, such as lighting the fires and fetching wine for them, and similar services, nor should they have Christian nursemaids to look after their children, nor should they have [Christian] livestock-drivers or gardeners or shepherds, nor should they approach or attend the celebrations or weddings or burials of Christians, nor should they become the godmothers or godfathers of Christians, nor should Christians be godparents to them, nor should they go to their weddings or burials or have any dealings with them concerning the above, on pain of 2,000 *maravedis*.

(10) Also that no male or female Jew or Moor should dare to visit a Christian in his or her illnesses or give them medicines or potions

---

* See introduction to chapter I.

[*jaropes*], nor should Jewish or Moorish men bathe in a [public] bath with the said Christian men, nor should they send them presents of puff pastries (*fojaldres*) or spices, or baked bread, or dead birds or any other dead meats or dead fish, or fruits or other dead things to eat. And anyone who goes against this and does the contrary, whether Jew or Moor, shall pay 300 *maravedis* for each offence.

(11) Also that no Christian woman, whether married or single, or a girlfriend [*amigada*] or a prostitute, should dare to enter into the enclosure [*cercado*] in which the said Jews and Moors live, by night or by day. And any Christian woman who does enter inside, if she is married, shall pay, for each offence of entering the enclosure, 100 *maravedis*, and if she is single, or [someone's] girlfriend, she should lose the clothes she was wearing [!], and, if she is a prostitute, she should be given a hundred lashes by the justices and thrown out of the city, town or village in which she lives.

(13) Also that no male Jews of my kingdoms and lordships, after ten days from now, should wear hoods with straps [*chías*] hanging down [a sign of nobility and authority at the time], unless they are strips no longer than a few inches [*un palmo*] made like a cone [symbol of a trickster, or *embudo*] or horn, sewn all round up to the point [of the hood]; also that that they should wear over their [other] clothes tabards with flaps [*aletas*], and that they should not wear capes [*mantones*, like canons' or academics' capes], and that they should wear their customary red badges as they do now, on pain of losing all the clothes they have on.

(14) Also that all the Jewish and Moorish women of my kingdoms and lordships, after the said ten days have passed, should wear large cloaks [*mantones*] down to their feet, without fine silk decoration and without feathers, and [should wear] headgear without gold [decoration], and should cover their heads with the folds of the aforesaid cloaks. And anyone who does the contrary shall thereby lose the clothes she is wearing, down to her undershirt [*camisa*], for each offence.

(18) Also that from now on none of the Jews and Moors of my kingdoms and lordships, should cut their beards or have them cut with a razor or scissors, but instead should wear them long, as they grow; neither should they trim or cut their hair; and that they should go about as they used to do in former times. And anyone who does the contrary should be given a hundred lashes and in addition should pay a hundred *maravedis* each time he does it.

(b) The Laws (*takkanot*) of Valladolid, 1432

[From *Fontes*, 5, pp. 93-7. See document 24 (ii)]

[Concerning Dress]

Inasmuch as in many communities [*kehillot*], may their Rock and Saviour guard them, there are dishonest and harmful rules and customs concerning the manner and dress of women, and their jewels, which are excessive and beyond what is proper: They wear very costly and flashy clothes, [including] both rich materials and rich objects, such as trains and gold and silver jewels and pearls, and rich adornments of fur, and many other things, which are the cause of much ill, [because] heads of families spend money and get into debt, so that in this way envy and hatred grow once more between the [Christian and Jewish] peoples, and they even think that they may rise to great wealth, in place of their poverty and misery, and abandon [the Jewish community]; yet, from time to time decrees are made for this reason against us, and, furthermore, we have never been considered entirely innocent, and it is right that we should make strong laws [*takkanot*] concerning this and should be strict in this matter.

Therefore we announce that no woman who is not a marriageable girl or a fiancée in the year of her marriage, should wear a saucy dress [lit. *de salsa*] of gold cloth or Chinese silk [*azeituni*] or taffeta, or silk, or fine leather [*chamelote*], nor should she wear decoration of fine [woollen] cloth, or Chinese silk, nor should she wear jewellery made of gold or pearls, or a band of pearls on the top of her forehead, or a train measuring more than a foot in length from any of her clothing.

And this statement is not to be understood to apply to the clothes which may be worn during festivals, or the reception of a lord or lady, or for dances or similar occasions things - things that everyone [*la generalidad*] is involved in. And inasmuch that there is great diversity amongst [Jewish] communities in matters of dress [so] that it would not be possible to make general laws, let it be sufficient to declare all the details which ought to be included in [such a law]. Therefore, we order that communities should make an ordinance among themselves on the aforementioned subject for the period of this law [of Valladolid], so that [Jewish] people may show restraint and realise that we are in the diaspora [expelled from the Land of Israel] because of our sins: and if they have the wish to be strict [with these women] beyond what is ordained here, they may do so.

Also, if, when anyone gets married or has a wedding, or has a child born to him [*sic*], as in other celebrations of that kind, they spend excessively, we agree that [local] communities should rule on the matter in the way that seems fitting to them, and in conformity with necessity and the situation.

32. Jewish dress and badges: Spain, 1491

Contained in a letter from Burgos city council to Ferdinand and Isabella, dated 2 December 1491, to Juan de Ribera, captain general of the frontier of Navarre, and the chief royal magistrates (*corregidores*) of Calahorra, Logroño and Alfaro, ordering them to implement earlier laws on dress and badges for Jews (Valladolid, 1412 and 1432)

[From Suárez Fernández, *Documentos,* pp. 377-9; in Spanish]

Also, most excellent lords, your highnesses know well how, according to the laws of your kingdoms, Jews and Moors have to wear on their clothes customary badges, by which they may be distinguished from Christians, and despite this we see that the Jews and Moors who are living in your kingdoms, or the majority of them, do not wear the said badges, but rather, some or others of them go about wearing such clothes and fine cloth and silks, and of such quality of manufacture ['*hechura*', or 'couture'] that it is impossible to know if the Jews are [indeed] Jews, or if they are clerics or lawyers of great estate and authority, and if the Moors are [indeed] Moors, or gentlemen of the palace, and they have gold and silver on their saddles and on their spurs and stirrups, and on their belts and swords. And how many injuries result and follow from this, apart from the offence that God receives from it. Wherefore we appeal to your highness [*sic*] to command and ordain that [neither] the Jews nor the Moors of your kingdoms should have gold or silver on their saddles and in their stirrups and spurs and swords, or wear silk or scarlet in their over or undergarments. And also that Jews and Moors should each wear their badge, the Moorish man his green hood covering his clothing, and the Jew or Jewess their round red badge on the right shoulder on the outside of their clothing, and Moorish women a blue patch on the right shoulder on the outside of their clothing, which should be four inches wide in the place where it appears. And your highnesses should revoke any letters which any Jews and Moors may have so that they do not have to wear badges. And either if they fail to wear them, or [else if] they hide them so that they do not appear publicly, or they have gold or silver on their saddles or on their stirrups or spurs or swords and belts or in any other such thing, for not wearing the said badge or wearing it concealed, or wearing silk or scarlet as has been said, they should lose their overgarments and that any person may strip them of it without penalty. [Also] for using harness [*jahezes e arreos*] with gold and silver they should lose [the harness], and anyone who can catch them with such things should take anything of this kind that he may find before the judge or magistrate of the place where this happens, so that he may award half to [the finder] and the other half to the judge who gives the sentence. But if the one who takes this clothing or harness from the Jew and Moor does not bring it immediately before the said judge or magistrate, he should be punished like one who commits violence, and the clothing and harness should be for the judge.

To this we respond that it pleases us and we grant and command that this should be implemented and kept henceforward in accordance with, and in the manner and under the penalties that by this petition you have asked of us.

33. Sunday travel by Jews: Spain, 1482

A letter on the subject from the Catholic Monarchs to their local authorities in Castile, dated at Valladolid on 30 April 1482, and containing an earlier document, issued in the same city on 28 April 1482.

[From Suárez Fernández, *Documentos*, pp. 261-3; in Spanish]

Don Ferdinand and Doña Isabella [etc.], to our chief justice and the *corregidores* and magistrates and judges and **merinos** and any other justices in the **merindades** of Carrión and Monzón and Saldaña and Campos, and the other cities and towns and villages of our kingdoms and lordships, and to each one of you to whom this letter may be shown, or else a copy of it sealed by a public scribe, salutation and grace.

Know that Moses Mañán, Jew, in the name of and as proctor of the Jewish communities of these our kingdoms of Castile and León, reported to us that you, or some of you, in order to annoy them and commit evils and damage, when they are travelling and going about their business, and doing so on Sundays and on festivals which the Church orders to be kept, and go along the roads, it is said that you, or some of you, have arrested them or had them arrested for travelling on the aforesaid Sundays and festivals, and have taken large quantities of *maravedis* from them. [Apparently you have told] them that they are not carrying lances seven 'elbows' in length [3 metres or 10 feet, approx.] on the roads, and because they were not carrying them, you extorted and took, and had taken, from them certain *maravedis*, claiming, it is said, that [this money] was the penalty you required for this. In all this it is said that, if it happened thus, they would receive great aggravation and harm, and other dangers and evils and injuries and inconveniences might arise for them in the future. And [the Jews] made supplication to us and asked for favour to be granted to them so that, since they have to work and seek their necessities even on Sundays and [Christian] festivals, and have to travel on the roads outside population centres [*poblados*], we should order provision to be made in this matter, and in each aspect of it, with remedy and with justice, giving an order and prohibition, with the effect that you may not take, or have taken or levied any *maravedis* from the said Jews or from any one of them, for travelling on Sundays and festivals, or because any of them were not carrying the aforementioned ten-foot long lances, [with the intention] that they may travel safely and look after their businesses and property, or else we shall provide in all this with justice, whatever our favour may be.

This [matter] having been examined in our council, it was agreed that we should order this our letter to be given for you in this sense, whereby we order each and every one of you, in your places and jurisdictions, to examine the above and everything in it, and [we order] that you should not, now or henceforward, force or constrain any Jews to carry the said lances if they do not wish to do so, and you should not take or levy from them any *maravedis* or other things for not carrying them, and you should allow and consent that they should travel freely on all the days on which they may wish to travel the roads, wherever they wish and understand it to be in their interest, and you should not molest them or allow or give occasion that because of [the above] or any part of it they should suffer extortion or be ill-treated, nor should any other evil or harm or injustice be done to them in their persons or in their goods or in anything of theirs, against reason and law, under those penalties and cases into which fall those who break a safeguard given by letter of their king and queen and natural law.

34. A Jewish kidnapping: Italy, 1434

A Christian is sentenced to death for murdering a Jewish banker's son, after kidnapping him and asking for a ransom. A Jew and two Christians were involved too. The sentence was carried out in the presence of the *podestà* of Perugia on 7 June 1434.

[From Ariel Toaff, *The Jews in Umbria*, vol. i, *1245-1435*, Leiden, 1993, pp. 449-54; in Italian]

In the name of God, amen.

This is the condemnation of the body and the corporal sentence published, given and in this document pronounced by way of a sentence and promulgated by the magnificent man [*per magnificum virum*] Simone, formerly of Bondeimonti and now of Monteboni in the territory of Florence, count of Grippefrancole, [who is] the honourable magistrate [*podestà*] of the city of Perugia and of its territory [*contado*], empowered by the Holy Roman Church and our most holy in Christ and lord pope Eugenius, by divine providence the fourth of that name and also by the magnificent and exalted people of Perugia. After the examination, council, deliberation and will of the highly learned in the law, Master Benedetto di Magnani of Arezzo and Master Batista di Riccobaldi of Volterra, [who are] among the honourable advisers of the aforesaid lord *podestà*, of all and each of the judges and assessors of the aforesaid lord *podestà*, [this sentence] was written, read, published and made known to the public [in Italian: *vulgarizata*] by me, Antonio Michele di Tignoselli of Volterra, public notary, and now especially deputed, among other things, as notary and official of crimes [*mallefitiorum*] of the aforesaid lord *podestà*.

In the year of Our Lord Jesus Christ 1434, in the twelfth year of the reign of the most holy in Christ, and father and lord on behalf of the Lord, Eugenius the fourth, by the divine providence pope, on the days and in the months written below.

We, Simon, formerly of Bondeimonti and now of Monteboni in Florentine lands, the aforesaid count and *podestà*, sitting in tribunal on our accustomed bench of criminal justice, as is usual, ... where such corporal condemnations are accustomed to be given, read and announced, hereby make the bodily condemnation and give sentence of condemnation in person written below, against Bartolomeo for the misdeeds, offences, excesses and crimes detailed below, which were done, said, committed and perpetrated by him, and in these writings and by sentence, we condemn, publish and announce in the form which follows.

Bartolomeo Pieri di Bononia, a treacherous man and vagabond, of bad condition, conversation, life and fame, and a public and manifest waster and kidnapper, was physically present to hear this, our corporal sentence, we having proceeded against him in proper form by the means and method of an enquiry, in, of and concerning that which referred to earlier public rumour and clamorous insinuation, not from malevolent and suspect persons, but rather from honest, truthful and trustworthy men and persons [*sic*], which came to the ears and notice of, and were heard by the aforesaid lord *podestà* and judges, not just occasionally but all the time. [That is to say that], in the present year and in the month of February of the aforesaid year, and in the month of February of that year, when this same Bartolomeo, together with Abraham Venture, a Jew from Rome, both inhabitants of Perugia, being in Castro Sant'Urbano, in the county of Narni, [we heard] from Pietro di Como, who was living in the aforesaid Castro, and stated that the aforementioned Abraham had succeeded in abducting Guglielmo Salamoni, a Jew of Arezzo, a boy aged about eleven, and that in such a way he brought it about that this same Pietro should kidnap the aforesaid Guglielmo, and having captured him, should bring him to whatever place was desired by this same Pietro. Also that the said Guglielmo would be released from the above in return for two thousand ducats from his father, the aforesaid Salomone, and these two thousand ducats should be stolen from him by force and violence, and that the same Guglielmo should be placed in the hands of the same Pietro, with this same Abraham receiving his share of the aforesaid two thousand ducats. Having heard these words from the aforesaid Pietro, the same Bartolomeo immediately, compelled by a diabolical spirit, from that time kept thinking about the above [plot], and made frequent efforts to put it into effect.

In this way, in the aforementioned year and in the month of April in the said year, this same Bartolomeo, living in the city of Perugia and seeing the abovementioned Abraham in the aforesaid city, so that he might better undertake his evil and iniquitous project, went, at the prompting of a diabolical spirit, to one Paghanino Giovanni di Milano, a citizen of the said city of Perugia, then living in that same city, and thus spoke to the same Paghanino about the above matters, since this same Paghanino agreed with the said Bartolomeo in everything concerning the committing, doing and perpetrating of the above [crime]. And at once, this same Bartolomeo and Paghanino went to the aforesaid Abraham, who was then living in the aforesaid city of Perugia, who, after many words which have already been mentioned, spoke with the aforesaid Bartolomeo and Paghanino concerning the aforementioned Guglielmo Salamoni.

And since the said Paghanino was afraid to go to the aforesaid city of Arezzo, the abovementioned Abraham, Bartolomeo and Paghanino, desiring to carry out their wicked project, decided to go to the city of

Siena to make contact with a certain Moses Isaac de Tibure, who was living there, and having thus discussed the matter with him, by thought and dealing, which were inspired by a diabolical spirit, not having God before their eyes but rather the enemy of the human race [the devil], craftily and with predetermined will and intention to commit and perpetrate the aforesaid crime, offence and excess, left the aforesaid city of Perugia and went to the aforesaid city of Siena. And when they were unable to fulfil their evil and iniquitous plan immediately in the aforesaid city of Siena, they decided to stay there, and did so, until the said Guglielmo, who had gone to the sea to bathe [*qui iverit ad balneas*], returned to that same city of Siena.

And when the said Abraham saw the abovementioned Guglielmo, he went to the said Bartolomeo and Paghanino and, having spoken with them, with thought and dealings, left them with the aforesaid and undermentioned mind and intention, and went to the said Guglielmo and persuaded him in such a way that he led him to the aforesaid Bartolomeo and Paghanino, who were standing and waiting with such a thought and intention for the said Abraham and Guglielmo, outside the gate of the aforesaid city of Siena. And in this way he handed over this same Guglielmo as a prisoner to the aforesaid Bartolomeo and Paghanino, who received him in the aforesaid way as a captive, with the mind and intention of having that same Guglielmo ransomed for the abovementioned two thousand ducats from the said Salamone his father, and that this same Salamone should be robbed by force and violence of the aforesaid two thousand ducats, and that the said Guglielmo, son of the same Salamone, should not be released until the said Salamone had been robbed and effectively despoiled of the aforementioned two thousand ducats. And as soon as the aforesaid Abraham brought the said Guglielmo, in the manner and form already described, to the abovementioned Bartolomeo and Paghanino, these same Bartolomeo and Paghanino put this same Guglielmo on the back of the horse that was being ridden by the aforesaid Paghanino, and at once, secretly, craftily and fraudulently, fled from there and headed for the abovementioned city of Arezzo, and in these circumstances came and brought the aforementioned Guglielmo to the aforesaid city of Perugia, to the place commonly known as 'Lo Scaffaio'....

They detained this same Guglielmo … for seventeen hours and more, in the county and jurisdiction of the aforesaid city of Perugia, and in order that they might in these circumstances better and more effectively bring the said Guglielmo to the field of military exercises [*ad campum gentis armorum*], in order the more easily to carry out their bad, evil and iniquitous project, in addition to the abovementioned seventeen hours, they kept him imprisoned and captured for twelve hours and more in that house in which the aforesaid Bartolomeo was and is caught in flagrant crime. And all the above was said, done, committed and perpetrated by the abovementioned Bartolomeo, Paghanino and Abraham, in the manner and form described above, in the year and months outlined above, and against the will of the aforesaid Guglielmo and Salamone and to their great harm, danger, prejudice and loss, and against the form of the law and statutes of the city of Perugia.

[There follows the sentence of death against the Christian, Bartolomeo Pieri.]

35. Separation of Jews from Christians: Spain, 1477, 1492; Italy, 1523

(a) A royal order to the local authorities in Soria, given in Seville, 28 December 1477

[From Suárez Fernández, *Documentos*, pp. 133-4; in Spanish]

Don Ferdinand and Doña Isabella [etc.]. To the *corregidor* and magistrates and any other justices in the town of Soria, and to each one to whom this letter may be shown, or else a copy of it, sealed by a public scribe, salutation and grace. Know that I the king, with the agreement of those in my Council and of certain grandees and prelates of our kingdoms, acting in conformity with their laws and ordinances, and believing it to be in accordance with the service of God and the progress of our holy faith, and to avoid the injuries which followed because Jews used to live and dwell among Christians, we ordain and command that from now on Jews should not live or dwell among Christians, as is stated more fully in certain of our letters which we order on this matter. And because it is our favour that [those letters] should be acted on and adhered to, we order each and every one of you that you immediately separate the said Jews from the said Christians and that they should move to the **Jewry**, and the designated place that is kept for them. And if in this aforesaid town [the Jews] do not have a separate place [of residence] from the Christians, you should immediately designate a suitable place for them to be in, and once houses and space have been made for them [there], from then on you should not allow them to exist and dwell among Christians any more. And so that the foregoing may be put into effect immediately, we are sending there [to you] our servant Velasco de Castroverde, to whom we give sufficient power so that he may immediately make [the Jews] separate from and abandon the Christians and live in their Jewry and separated place, and so that he may force them, and do this quickly, and in order to carry out the penalties that have been placed on them by us if they do not act thus and comply in this.

(b) A Royal letter to the corregidor of Guipúzcoa, Juan de Ribera, continuing earlier policy towards Jews, but given on 17 March 1492, only a fortnight before the expulsion edict was framed.

[From: Suárez Fernández, *Documentos*, pp. 389–91; in Spanish]

Don Ferdinand and Doña Isabella [etc.]. Know that on the part of Yusef del Corral, citizen in the town of Logroño, it was reported to us in our Council that in the town of Laguardia, two leagues from the said city [of Logroño], there was an argument in the said town over the separation [*apartamiento*] of Christians from Jews, and it was stated that in the end, to avoid expense and labours, the said debate was put into the hands and power of certain persons, who gave a sentence in which they ordered that the said Jews should live on the main street, on either side of some houses which belonged at the time to Pedro Martínez de Berunda, with the said passageway from one side to the other, so as to be joined to the said Jewry, in order to live and dwell in the said houses, since between the said houses which he had bought in the aforesaid way from the said Pedro Martínez, there was no Christian house or property. It is said that in these houses, a son of the said Yusef lived for the space of ten years and more, without any dispute, and it is said that now some people in the aforesaid town, through anger and ill-will which they have against the said Yusef, will not consent or allow that the said Yusef or any other Jew should live or dwell in the said houses, because these houses were not involved in the separation [*apartamiento*] which was made by virtue of the said sentence of arbitration. Also, in the case that he were given leave to live in the aforesaid houses, they would not allow him to be in the aforesaid passage, as he always was [before].

[Yusef petitioned the monarchs to put the houses concerned into the separated Jewish quarter of the *apartamiento*, which they duly did, a mere fortnight before issuing their edict of expulsion]

(c) Commission and mandate from Pope Adrian VI to Cristòfero Spiriti, bishop of Cesena, to force the Jews of that town to move to quarters separate from those of the Christians and forbid them to acquire any further property. Dated at Rome, 31 July 1523.

[From Simonsohn, *Documents:1522-1538*, pp. 1629-30; in Latin]

Pope Adrian VI.

Venerable brother, greetings and apostolic blessing. We have recently heard from our beloved sons, the [papal] officials, council and commune of our city of Cesena, who are concerned with the safety of the inhabitants and citizens of the aforesaid towns, and to avoid scandals, which will result if provision is not made [by us] concerning this matter, that it is expedient that the Jews, a large number of whom at present live among those citizens, should be taken away to another part of the city, where they may live separately, as is proper, and that they should be forbidden to acquire immovable property. The afore-mentioned officials, council and commune have appealed to us to deign to provide appropriately in this matter, out of our apostolic good will. We therefore, being inclined towards this petition, by these presents commit to you, our brother, and command that you should immedi-ately consign these Jews to whatever part of that town may be convenient and suitable for them, and that, if they wish to remain in the aforesaid town, you should, if necessary, coerce and compel them to live within the boundaries in which you arrange and agree that they should live. Also, you should prevent them from acquiring any houses or vineyards or fields, or any immovable goods elsewhere.... Given at Rome in St Peter's, under the **Fisherman's** ring, on the last day of July, 1523, in the first year of our **pontificate**.

36. Attempted starvation of Jews: Spain, 1484

Ferdinand and Isabella order their officials in Soria to assure provisions to the town's Jews who were living, on royal orders, in the castle (21 August 1484).

[From Suárez Fernández, *Documentos*, pp. 228-30; in Spanish]

Don Ferdinand and Doña Isabella [etc.], to you, the knights and town council, justices, councillors [*regidores*], squires, officials and good men of the noble city of Soria, salutation and grace.

Know that Jorge de Beteta, our **vassal**, and governor of the fortress and castle of this said city made report to us by means of his petition which he presented, saying that, recently and in fact ['*nuevamente de fecho*'], and against all reason and law, you have ordered and [issued] a prohibition in the said city, so that none or any persons may take up, or have taken up, provisions to the Jews ... [both] citizens [*vecinos*] and dwellers [*moradores*] [of or in Soria], who live and dwelt [*sic*] in the said fortress and castle. [Also] that you have made a certain ordinance concerning this, which is said to be to our disservice and greatly harmful to the said Jews, because the said Jews who live and dwell thus in the said fortress and castle are there for its defence and guard, and do a great deal of good in the guarding of the said fortress and castle. And it is said that, if the above were to come into effect, it would perforce happen that the said fortress and castle would be depopulated and the said Jews would go down to live in the said city, or would go to live in the kingdoms of Aragon or Navarre to seek their subsistence. Therefore, for the sake of what concerned our service, [Jorge de Beteta] notified us of the above and, for himself and in the name of the said Jews, made supplication to us and asked for our favour so that we should order provision to be made for them concerning the remedy of this matter with justice, commanding that the said ordinance thus made by you concerning the above be declared null [and void], and also ordering the lifting of any penalties that you may have placed on any persons who carried and took up provisions to the said castle, and also ordering you that, from now on, you should not impose the said prohibition, or make the said ordinance [again], or make use of it, under great penalties, or whatever our royal favour may be. And we found this to be good.

Therefore we order you that you should hold the said ordinance to be null, which you thus made concerning the above, and now and henceforward you should not employ it again, and thus you should not [issue] orders [against] or forbid any person or persons to take up or carry the said provisions to the said Jews who inhabit the said fortress and castle of this said city, and you should give back to them, and have lifted all and any penalties which you have imposed concerning this matter on these said persons, and you should allow them to go up and carry to the said fortress and castle the said provisions, accordingly and in the manner in which they took and carried them up before you made the said ordinance and put on the said ban. And you should not go against this [order] in any way on pain of our favour and of 10,000 *maravedis* each for our Chamber and Exchequer.

37. Racial laws against Jewish Christians: Spain, 1449; Portugal [undated]

(a) The 'Sentence-Statute' (*Sentencia-Estatuto*) of Pero Sarmiento, Toledo 5 June 1449. During a rebellion in Toledo, against the Castilian government of John II, a law was passed by those who had briefly usurped power in the city. Although rapidly repealed, once the Crown regained control, this legislation was to be the prototype of many more measures of the kind, in Spain and elsewhere.

[From Eloy Benito Ruano, *Los orígenes del problema converso*, Barcelona, 1976, pp. 89-90; in Spanish]

We must and do declare, must pronounce and do pronounce and constitute and ordain and command that all the said converts, descendants of the perverse lineage of the Jews, in whatever guise they may be, both by virtue of canon and civil law, which determines against them in the matter declared above [exclusion from public office], and by virtue of the privilege given to this city by the said lord king of blessed memory, Don Alfonso, king of Castile and León, progenitor of the king our lord, and by other lords and kings their progenitors, and by his highness [the present king], sworn and confirmed as follows:

Since by reason of the heresies and other offences, insults, seditions and crimes committed and perpetrated by them up to this day ... they should be had and held, as the law has and holds them, as infamous, unable, incapable and unworthy to hold any office and public or private **benefice** in the said city of Toledo and in its land, territory and jurisdiction, through which they might have lordship over Christians who are old believers [*sic*] in the holy Catholic faith of Our Lord Jesus Christ, to do them harm and injury, and thus be infamous, unable and incapable to give testimony on oath as public scribes or as witnesses, and particularly in this city; and by this, our sentence and declaration, following the tenor and form of the said privilege, liberties, franchises and immunities of the said city, we deprive them, and declare them to be and order that they be deprived of whatever offices and benefices they have had and held in this said city, in whatever manner.

(b) A letter certifying the 'cleanliness of birth' of Jorge de Oliveira, esquire of the royal household and receiver of monies in the royal Chancellery. Undated, but early sixteenth century

[From Maria José Pimento Ferro Tavares, *Judaísmo e Inquisição. Estudos* (Lisbon, 1987), pp. 192-3; in Portuguese]

Dom Manuel [etc.].... To whomsoever may see this our letter, we make it known that we, having respect for the upbringing that the princess, my lady mother, has given to Jorge de Oliveira, esquire of our household and receiver [of monies] in the chancellery of our Court, and therefore, as he is one who deserves it, we hold it good and it pleases us that no criminal or civil ordinances, policies, public pronouncements and customs, that have been made by us and by our officials or that we may make in the future, are to be understood [as going] against the said Jorge de Oliveira and his wife and children. And, as we said [previously], we remove and annul all these [acts] on their behalf. And it pleases us, and we hold it good, that he and his aforesaid children may be called 'New Christians', and we remove from them and annul all and every stain that, because of their birth, may be alleged against them, because we discovered there was [no such stain]. Therefore it pleases us and is our wish that he should be able to do and say everything, as because of his birth it is not forbidden to him under any laws and ordinances which have been or may be made to the contrary, because we wish that none of them should have force against this our letter, and it pleases us that the said Jorge de Oliveira, being our servant and an official in our chancellery, should have and enjoy all the honours, privileges and liberties that all our other receivers in the said chancellery possess, which we desire should be completely kept for him; and thus we order the head of our house of [criminal] appeals and the governor of our civil court, and all our **corregedores** and justices, that they should, in everything and for every purpose, comply with and keep this our letter, as is contained within it, because this is our favour.

38. Ritual murder accusations: the story of Simon of Trent, Italy, 1475

Papal intervention in the case of the accusation of ritual murder made against the Jews of Trent, in northern Italy, in 1475. A letter from Sixtus IV to two bishops, dated in Rome, on 30 December 1480

[From Simonsohn, *1464-1521*, pp. 1276-78; in Latin]

Sixtus, [etc.].... To our venerable brothers, Angelo of Feltre, presently living in the city of Vicenza, and Pietro of Cattaro, bishops, greeting.... Since the greatest matters are known to require the greatest scrutiny and investigation, and also the great intelligence and instruction of prudent men, in such a matter [as the murder of Simon] it is necessary that the Roman pontiff, who, because of the resistance of human nature, cannot carry out his duty by himself, according to the exigency of matters, employs his fellow bishops, whom the Most High has called to a share of [his] pastoral care, particularly in difficult and serious matters, with equal strength and diligence.

Some while ago, when our beloved son the magistrate of the city of Trent, responding to public rumour, as the seriousness of the matter required and was demanded of his office, undertook an investigation into certain Jews residing in that same city, who had inhumanly killed a Christian child. He sentenced those found guilty to the ultimate penalty [death], and on this account many serious men began to murmur, and the matter [began] to be viewed in various places with hostile suspicion. We, in order that every occasion of such suspicion should be removed, will both carry out the duty [imposed by] our pastoral office, and also, so that the truth of the deed should be known to all the faithful, ended the magistrate's [legal] process against the aforesaid Jews, and thereafter [the case] was sent [to us] by our venerable brother John, bishop of Trent, provided with his [episcopal] seal and that of our nuncio.

We had [the case] carefully inspected and examined by some of our venerable brothers, cardinals and archbishops of the Holy Roman Church, referrers and auditors of causes in the Apostolic palace. After frequent meetings, having examined every part of this process, and having proceeded in this case in due and correct form, they faithfully referred it back to our Consistory. We, then, being at one with these our brothers, and feeling in the same way as them about the above account, and commanding, in the Lord, the study and diligence [in this matter] of the said John, bishop of Trent, wish, and have attached [to this document] some other letters, so that he should not permit his pious and irregular devotion of the faithful. This accords with [the terms] of the decretal of Pope Innocent III, of blessed memory issued in general council [Lateran IV], that anything that is illicitly attempted, which may bring injury to God and contempt to the Apostolic See, or any other things which are done without possibility of excuse against canonical sanctions, are to be stopped. Concerning this [matter], our conscience has been burdened, in what has been entrusted to us by the Lord. Since, however, it is asserted by some that a great gathering of people from different areas has begun to assemble in the church in which the body of the said child is kept, and, according to the evidence of public rumour, many miracles have been shown forth there, we, having waited for some time to see whether these miracles are true and undoubted, and to discern their reasons and causes and find out all about them, and [also] so that this business might be dealt with most seriously and maturely, and trusting greatly in your prudence, integrity and doctrine, and having also taken the advice of our brothers [the investigators], already referred to, we commit to you and order you, by virtue of holy obedience and by

apostolic letters, laying aside every affection, but pursuing the pure
and naked truth, and having God alone before your eyes, by our
authority, jointly to inform us with diligence, about this public fame
and devotion of the faithful, whether they have their origin in the
weighty opinions of the wise, or in the simplicity of the people, or in
other numerous and diverse causes, by which the omnipotent God
makes miracles occur. Having examined suitable witnesses, the most
serious and trustworthy men, individually and secretly, a burden
which we place on your consciences, after they have sworn an oath in
your hands, you should have their statements and depositions collected in writing by a public and reliable notary, and you should ensure
that the process carried out by you concerning them should be sent to
us in public, collected and complete form, and sealed with your
[episcopal] seals, by a trustworthy and faithful messenger, and we
rely on you to provide in these matters with your [full] diligence, fully
informed, correctly and properly. And, so that you may accomplish the
above with greater ease, by these presents [i.e. this document] we
grant a full and free faculty to you and to any [other] Christian
believers, whether they be secular or ecclesiastical persons, with the
remedies of ecclesiastical and other laws, so that you may constrain
and compel witnesses to testify concerning the above.

39. Ritual murder accusations: the story of the 'Holy Child' of La Guardia, Spain, 1491

Documents of the Inquisition trial held in Avila in 1490-1491

[From Fidel Fita, 'La verdad sobre el martirio del Santo Niño de la Guardia,
o sea el proceso y quema (16 noviembre 1491) del judío Juçe Franco en Avila',
Boletín de la Real Academia de la Historia, XI (1887), pp. 7-160; in Spanish]

(a) From the statement of charges [*demanda*] presented against Juçe Franco
by the **procurator fiscal** of the Avila tribunal of the Inquisition, Alonso de
Guevara, on 17 December 1490. The trial took place in the home town of the
inquisitor-general, Tomás de Torquemada.

[Fita, 'La verdad', pp. 12-14]

Most virtuous and reverend lords. I, **bachelor** Alonso de Guevara,
procurator fiscal of the Holy Inquisition in this city of Avila and its
diocese, appear before you, reverend fathers, in the best way that I can,
and I denounce and charge Yuçe Franco, Jew, citizen of Tembleque,
who is present. Who, not content that, through humanity alone, he
with all the other Jews are allowed, according to our faith, and allow

themselves to live and have dealings with faithful and Catholic Christians, induced and attracted some Christians to his accursed law, with false and deceptive sermons and suggestions, just like an abettor of heretics, telling them and demonstrating to them that the law of Moses was the true one and the one by which they would be saved, and that [the law] of Jesus Christ was a made up and pretend law, and that no such law was imposed or enacted by God.

Item. He contracted and made a contract and agreement, as principal, jointly with others, to secure a consecrated host to commit outrages against it and abuse it, in vituperation of and contempt for our holy Catholic Faith, and because among the said Jews, accomplices in the aforesaid offence and conspiracy, there were certain sorcerers [*hechizeros*] and, on a day during their **Passover**, he had to receive the aforesaid host in communion [*sic*], and also the heart of a Christian child: and when these acts had been done in the aforesaid form and manner, all the Christians were to die of rabies. And the intention which moved Yuçe Franco and his followers and co-conspirators in the aforesaid agreement, was that the law of Moses should be better honoured and kept, and that its rites and precepts and ceremonies be more freely kept by them, and because the entire Christian religion would perish and be subverted, and they [the Jews] would possess all the goods that the Catholic and faithful Christians have and possess, and no-one would come to contradict their evils and perverse errors, and their generation would grow and multiply on the earth, the faithful Christians having been completely eliminated.

Item. He committed other offences and cases concerning the Holy Office of the Holy Inquisition [unspecified].

(b) From the reply by Martín Vázquez, the legal representative [*procurador*] of Yuçe Franco, who delivered his objections to the prosecution case in Avila on 22 December 1490

[Fita, 'La verdad', pp. 17-18]

The first [objection] is inasmuch as [the prosecution statement] is vague and obscure; because, in his denunciation [the prosecutor] does not state, express or clarify the places, or the years, or the months, or the days, or the times or the persons, in which and with whom he says that the aforesaid, my part [i.e. client] committed the offences of which he accuses him, nor those who surrounded [*los linderos de*] the said places ... But it is not right that, in the case of my client, who, being a Jew, cannot properly or truly be said to have committed a crime of heresy or apostasy, the expression of what accusations are made against him personally should cease or not be made clear, since my client is favoured in this matter by the great equity and goodwill of the Church, and hence [that] of you, reverend fathers. Since it is a most certain and often proved thing that without that [equity and goodwill], my aforesaid client cannot defend himself properly, or know anything about what he is accused of, because of the generality and obscurity of the said booklet [libello] of charges. And it is a thing very much against law that the aforesaid prosecutor, in so great prejudice of my client, should not give details of his accusations against him. And from the generalized nature of [his accusations] there could result some prejudice to your consciences, reverend fathers, if my client should suffer and die undefended, and your justice, in the aforesaid 'solid' [funditus] cause should perish. Since, if some laws dispose that in a case of heresy, if it is committed secretly, an inquisition or book of accusations is valid [even] without details of time and place, they are understood [to apply] and restricted to cases in which the crime of heresy has truly been committed, which is not the case with my client. This is because, being a Jew, without a truly and properly baptized soul, he could not commit the aforesaid offence, or be denounced for heresy, nor did he do or commit anything, whereby the aforesaid crime [the 'ritual murder'] was committed. For which reasons I ask you, reverend fathers, in the name of the aforesaid Jew, to reject the aforesaid accusation, or at least to order the aforesaid prosecutor to clarify and give details of his charges, and in particular to clarify and give details of his charges, so that they may be properly understood, and my client may defend himself properly, and put forward his righteousness, and prove the contrary if he should so wish. Otherwise, I ask your graces to reject the aforesaid accusation; if you do not, I protest about my complaint [quexa] to whomever the law requires, and above all I place the responsibility on the consciences of your graces.

[The rest of this statement is a straightforward denial of the charges]

(c) Revealing evidence concerning the *converso* Benito García, from the testimony of Yuçe Franco, given in Avila on 9 April 1491. *Çapatera* and *presión de abaxo* are euphemisms for tortures.

[Fita, La verdad', pp. 34–5]

Yuçe Franco, Jew, a sworn witness, under oath, said that he had begun to talk to Benito García, who is a prisoner in the Inquisition's prison in Avila, under the same imprisonment in which this witness is placed. And, once they were [both] imprisoned, they began to talk. And the aforesaid Benito García would say, 'Jew, do you have a needle you could give me?' And this witness said to him that he did not have a needle but he was on the shoemaker's last [*çapatera*]. And this witness said to him, 'Where is he?' And the aforesaid Benito replied, 'In this pressure from below [*presión de abaxo*] And you know that your father, Don Isaac Franco, is there'. And this witness said that [his father] could not be there. And the aforesaid Benito answered that he had seen him, because the fathers [of the Inquisition] had him brought up so that he [Benito] could go and see if he knew who he was. And that this witness [Yuçe] asked him who this Benito was, and [his father, Don Isaac] replied that he was García the woolcarder, who was 'bad news' [*en ora mala*], and that the devil had brought him here; and dog of a doctor [Pedro de Villada], who had given him two hundred lashes in Astorga, and also water torture, and on another night two partial stranglings [*garrotes*], so that they might discover the other people with whom they would burn him. And while this witness was playing a guitar [*vihuela*], the aforesaid García would say to him, in an undertone, 'Don't play that [instrument], have pity on your father, as the inquisitors have said that they must burn him, little by little'. And this witness [Yuçe Franco] asked him if he was a *converso*. And the aforesaid Benito García replied that he was a *converso*, and had even been a Jew, in a bad time [*en ora mala*]; and that he commended himself to the prayers of this Jewish witness, so that the Creator might deliver them from that oppression; although he had only a bad cure to offer, because 'under torture he had said more than he knew'.

(d) The sentence announced against Yuçe Franco at an *auto de fe* in Avila on 16 November 1491

[Fita, 'La verdad', pp. 100-1, 105-6]

And they [the inquisitors] pronounced and had read [publicly] a sentence, written on paper, the tenor of which from word to word [*de verbo ad verbum*, i.e. literally] is as follows:

✝ Jesus. There having been seen and diligently examined by us, Dr Pedro de Villada, abbot of San Millán and San Marcial in the churches of Burgos and León, and Brother Fernando de Santo Domingo, a professor of the Order of Preachers [Dominicans], judge inquisitors of heretical depravity and apostasy in the city of Avila and in its entire diocese, and in the same way especially deputed in the present case by apostolic authority [i.e. the papacy], and also being, as we are, ordinary judges in the aforesaid case for the most reverend lord Don Pedro González de Mendoza, Cardinal of Spain, Archbishop of Toledo, primate of the Spains, a process and case which remains pending and undecided before us between parties, that is to say, the one prosecuting, the honourable bachelor Alonso de Guevara, procurator fiscal [*promotor fiscal*] of this Holy Inquisition, and on the other side, the prisoner being prosecuted, Yuçe Franco, Jew, citizen and inhabitant of Tembleque, in the archdiocese of Toledo, and which concerns a petition that the aforesaid prosecutor initiated and lodged before us against the aforesaid Yuçe Franco, Jew, and certain additions to the said petition, also provided by the aforementioned prosecutor, whereby he said that the aforesaid Yuçe Franco, Jew, had induced some Christians and attracted them to his Law, and similarly was an abettor of heretics, giving them to understand that the Law of Christ was made up and simulated, and that the Law of Moses was the true one [the sentence then repeats all the earlier charges]....

Christ's name having been invoked, we find that we must pronounce sentence and declare, and do pronounce, sentence and declare, that the intention of the aforesaid prosecutor is well and sufficiently proved and verified; and that the aforesaid Yuçe Franco, Jew, did not prove anything which could relieve or help him. With the result that we must and do declare him to be an active abettor and participant in the crime and offence of heresy and apostasy, and an obstructor of the Holy Office of the Inquisition, and subverter of the Christian faith and Law, and inducer of Christians to deny the aforesaid law of Jesus Christ our Redeemer and receive that of Moses; being a participant in the aforesaid crimes and offences together with Christians; and for this [we declare him] to have fallen into and incurred all the temporal penalties and confiscation and loss of all his goods, established and imposed against such [offences] by the canon and civil law. And as such we must relax and do relax him to justice and the secular arm, to that honourable and noble man, the licentiate Alvaro de Santisteban, *corregidor* in this city of Avila and its lands for the most serene king and queen, our lords, and to his magistrates, constables and officials, so that they may do to the aforesaid Yuçe Franco, Jew, what they ought to do by law, applying the aforesaid his goods, which we declare to be confiscated and applied by law, to the chamber and exchequer [*cámara e fisco*] of the aforesaid most serene king and queen, our lords. And by this our definitive sentence, [given] by a tribunal in session [*pro tribunali sedendo*], we thus pronounce and sentence.

[After this, Yuçe Franco admitted, in front of witnesses, that he was guilty as charged. He then made a further confession at the stake, but this was not to be the end of the story. It was not long before a burial place was found for the non-existent 'holy child'. Firstly, on 18 November 1491, the sacristan of the church in La Guardia, Juan, son of Gómez del Alcázar, was interrogated by the inquisitors in Avila, and stated that, in November 1489, he had been asked for consecrated hosts [eucharistic bread] by Alfonso Franco, the sacristan's uncle, who was prepared to offer clothing and cash in return. According to this account, the sacristan gave a single host to Alfonso Franco, who handed it on to the wool-carder Benito García. On the day before, 17 November 1491, Gabriel Sánchez, a citizen of Avila who was also in the Inquisition's prison there, gave a statement to the tribunal that had just had Yuçe Franco burned.]

(e) Gabriel Sánchez's statement

[Fita, La verdad', pp. 111-12]

And Gabriel Sánchez, citizen of Avila, who is a prisoner in the aforesaid gaol, sworn in as a witness in the form of law [etc.], in Avila, on Thursday 17 November 1491, said that one night, about an hour after midnight, this witness saw and heard how Juan de Ocaña and Juan Franco were talking to each other in the aforesaid gaol. And that the aforesaid Juan Franco asked the aforesaid Juan de Ocaña what he had said [to the inquisitors], and that the said Juan de Ocaña replied to him and said that he had said [to the inquisitors] that the child was from Toledo and that he had white baby-clothes [*mantillas*], and that the aforesaid Juan Franco had carried him off, and that they crucified him in some caves in *Carre-Ocaña*, and that they had buried him in some gullies [*sic*], and that he named the place in which they buried him, but this witness does not remember it. [He also stated that] the aforesaid Juan Franco said, 'I said pretty much the same, but if they try to find out where the lad is buried, one will go here and the other will go there'. And this witness further says that the abovementioned had said that [various other named Jews and converts] had been with those who crucified the aforesaid lad.

[Thus it was that post-trial documents, rather than the Inquisition's trial of Yuçe Franco, provided some basis for the lurid sixteenth-century account of the affair which follows.]

(f) A later account: Spain, 1533

[From: Sebastián de Horozco, *La historia del niño inocente de La Guardia* [1533], ed. Jack Weiner, in *Relaciones históricas toledanas* (Toledo, 1981), pp. 29-38; in Spanish]

Very true memorial of the passion and martyrdom which was suffered by the glorious martyr and innocent child called Christopher, in the rooms or caves known as the Innocent's [caves], which are in [the territory of] this town of La Guardia, outside the walls, as will be stated below at greater length in the account or substance of the trial of Benito García, the great wool-carder, or De las Mesuras [measures], a heretical Jew and condemned, and of the rest which was and truly happened, and of eleven Jews who were present. It was this Benito who placed the crown [of thorns] on the head of, and took the heart from, the holy innocent child, in hatred and vengeance of Our Lord Jesus Christ, and in His place, not being able to attack Him, and the beginning of [Benito's] damned intention, known and established by true information, was as follows.

Certain Jews, some of those who were involved in the crucifixion of this blessed child and others who were not to be present at it, being in the kingdom of France, these Jews, it being believed that they were among those who fled from Castile when the king, Don Ferdinand, and the queen, Doña Isabella, Catholic Monarchs of blessed memory, constituted and ordained the Holy Inquisition, announcing that all the Jews who were in their kingdoms should be baptized and become Christians, or else leave them within a certain period. Many Jews, damned with evil hearts, gathered in France, looking for a way in which they could revenge themselves on the Christians.... It was revealed to them by diabolical revelation, or by the advice of some Jewish sage, or rather sorcerer ... that, taking the heart of an innocent boy, without sin, and the most Holy Sacrament of the altar, all burnt and reduced to dust, and thrown into the water which the Christians would drink, as soon as they drank it they would go mad and die. And in this way they would be revenged.

[To obtain the heart, the Jews supposedly suborned a poor French nobleman, with many children and little with which to support them, promising him great wealth if he would give them the heart of one of his sons. The nobleman's wife persuaded him to counter with a trick.]

The woman, being astute, and also because women, as may be seen by experience, or by their nature, are accustomed to giving very clear and useful advice, replied, almost without need for thought, 'Sir, do not worthy, I'll tell you how we can fool these Jews, without your killing your son and without their realizing it'…. We have this sow, which is small. Take it and kill it, and we'll take out its heart, and we'll say it comes from our son, and we'll have to hide our son, so that he won't be found. [After speaking to the Jews], this man went home and, as the woman had advised him, killed his sow, took its heart out and gave it to the Jews. They, when they saw the heart, really believing that it was the child's, took it with great delight, and they paid the nobleman a lot of money, with which he escaped easily from his misery.

Having already got the heart, it remained for them to find a way of getting hold of the most Holy Sacrament, and as they could not find it [for themselves], they agreed to secure their goal as follows. They wanted to have [the Eucharistic host] complete, just as it was in the tabernacle…. They thought up this ruse. Near them, there lived an old woman who was very poor, much poorer than the nobleman, and they went to her and said, 'Sister, it will be well worth your while to do what we are going to ask you. [They offered her the bribe of a piece of cloth]. The poor old thing said that, if she could, she would willingly do it. They said to her, 'You must go to communion, and when they give you the host, find a way of not eating it, don't swallow it, but get it to stick to the roof of your mouth, or else pretend to clean yourself with your hand and take it out of your mouth and keep it. Bring it to us, and we'll give you the cloth, and even more if you want it'…. So when the accursed old woman went on another day to receive [holy] communion, she found a way to bring the most holy sacrament to the Jews, who took it and kept it to do spells with it…. And they paid the diabolical old woman what they had promised, and much more, so that she would keep all this secret.

Having now searched for what they wanted to make their spell, the heretics [Jews or *conversos*] burnt to dust both the pig's heart, which they thought was a boy's, and the most Holy Sacrament, and went and threw [the result] into the passing river, to infect or bewitch all the water or waters which the Christian people used for drinking, so that when they drank it they would all die…. These Jews, or some of them, or some of their descendants, having returned to Castile, and being now Christians at least in name, sought to return to and finish their evil deed… They looked through Castile for a suitable place, one which in location and appearance resembled Jerusalem, and it seems that they found no place more suited to their purpose than this town of La Guardia. And for this purpose there was, it seems, in Avila or in the area of Avila, a Jewish rabbi, a great scholar, or rather a great sorcerer, to whom went these bad Christians and heretics, called the Francos [Franks], who were four brothers or relatives and other companions, eleven in all, and with them an accountant [*contador*] of the Order of Saint John of Jerusalem, a citizen of Tembleque, a person of great style and authority, who was to be the Pilate who gave the sentence like a robber....

These Francos were citizens and dwellers in this town of La Guardia, with their wives and children and property, and their businesses: they were carters. And, going to Toledo and back, they succeeded in finding or hearing of a blind woman who had a little son aged about seven or eight, called Christopher [Christovalico: 'little Christopher']. And they found a trick and way to get hold of the child with gifts, giving him some red booties. And the child, in his innocence, went off with them, because he liked what they gave him. And in this way they stole the son from the poor blind woman, his mother... For certain, it is an amazing thing and it moves hearts to tears of compassion to see how far they took the child, giving him blows with the cross on his back, and [this cross] so thick and solid as it must have been, and such a bitter thing when it is known that he received, on account of the accursed Jews, 6200 strokes.... And they gave him a thousand strokes more than they gave Christ, as was discovered from the confession of the aforesaid Jews.

The poor blind woman, mother of this holy child martyr ... had never seen light. And at the moment when her son died, at that very point, she received her sight... The aforesaid Jews, after they had crucified the child and extracted his heart, went to bury him deeply, almost a quarter of a league from the spot, close by a hermitage called Our Lady of Pera, doing all this very secretly at night, so as not to be noticed. After they had buried and laid to rest the body of the holy child, the aforesaid heretics decided to look for a way of getting hold of the most holy sacrament, as they did for the first time in France. And for this they dared to speak to one Juan de Gómez, who was a citizen of the aforesaid town of La Guardia [and] who today has a brother in the aforesaid town. This Juan de Gómez was, at the time, the sacristan of the church in the aforesaid town, and they asked him if he would give them the most holy sacrament of the altar, [saying that] they would give him a hood [in return]. This sacristan, looking to his own interest and [behaving] like a bad Christian, and no less a heretic and Jew than the others, found a way, with all cunning, to steal the most holy sacrament. He found an opportunity to do so because the priest happened to leave [the consecrated hosts] on the altar, or else give them to the sacristan to keep, and thus he must have taken the keys of the tabernacle in order to steal it. And having stolen it, he took it home and gave it to the aforesaid Jews. And [in return] they gave him a Courtrai hood, suborned, which had cost thirty [silver] *reales*, the same as the thirty pieces for which Christ was sold by Judas.

Having now got all that they wanted, that is, the most holy sacrament and the heart of an innocent boy, sinless like Christ and called Christopher, representing Our Lord also in his name, they sent one of their number, believed to be the aforesaid Benito García de las Mesuras, or one of the Francos, with all this to Avila or thereabouts, to take counsel as to how they were to do and achieve [their aim], because, as has already been said, there was a learned Jew [there] to do it and give advice about it.... This Jew, who was carrying the two relics, that is to say, the most holy sacrament and the heart of the holy child, staying as he did in the lodging-house or inn, the first thing he did was to go and pray in the Cathedral, and he carried the most holy sacrament between the pages of a book of hours, and the heart he left in safe-keeping in the lodging-house, wrapped in some cloths and locked in a knapsack. Once there, and saying his prayers as he was, this bad Christian opened his book of hours and, kneeling low on his knees, with his hands together, and beating his breast like the most devoted and Catholic man in the world, he noticed a man come in and kneel behind him. And while [the Jew] was praying, this [other] man saw, coming out of the book of hours with which this Jew was pretending to pray, things like flames, now green, now yellow, now various colours. The man, seeing that this was not natural, thought and believed with certainty that the Jew was in fact a very holy man. And [the Christian] kept his eye on [the Jew], so that he did not let him out of his sight, following him to his lodgings, where he entered, though the Jew was unaware of his presence. Having seen that [the Jew] was safely back in his lodgings, [the Christian] could do no other than run and tell the fathers of the Holy Inquisition, not with the thought that any harm would come to [the Jew] from it, but believing with certainty that he must be some holy man. And the Lord permitted it to be thus, that those accursed ones should not carry out their plan, but rather should pay for their evil magic.

When [the Christian] told the fathers of the Holy Inquisition, they asked the man whether what he told them was true. He replied, 'Yes, without any mistake, I saw a thousand splendours coming from him, and now he is staying in such and such a place'. The reverend fathers of the Holy Inquisition said to him, 'Well, take us there'. And the aforesaid man took them: and having been taken there they went in. And when they went in, the Jew's tongue was loosened straight away and when they began asking him questions, he began to give way, and confess the whole business from beginning to end, without their needing to torture him at all [*sic*]. Having confessed [himself] he said who all the others were who entered into this monopoly and business, and when [the inquisitors] knew of their evil and heresy, they put him under strict guard. And they then came to La Guardia and gave orders that, when [the conspirators] were at mass on a festival (since, pretending to be very holy and good Christians, they never missed mass or vespers, and did everything required of good Christians, although it was all false), the justices should come in, shut the doors [of the church] and arrest the others. In the end, none of them escaped arrest, either there or in their houses. And they were taken under close guard to Avila. And they were all kept separately, as is the custom of the Holy Inquisition, in order to know the truth and take their statements and confessions.

And it is certain that for seven or eight months, they did not know that the one who had taken the heart and the most holy sacrament was in prison. And during all this time, [the inquisitors] never discovered anything from the questions they asked them or the tortures they gave them. And so that none of them would confess the truth, one of them sang very loudly a song for the others to hear, which went, 'Hold on to the branch, little girl, you'll see, hold on to the branch and you won't die', and another song which went, 'Little castle, be strong for me, and I'll not be afraid of death'. Being all this time in the state of not having confessed, it happened [*sic*] that they found out about the one who had been arrested first, whom they had not known or believed to be there, and when they saw him they thought it was impossible that he had not confessed the truth. And when they confessed they were sentenced to the fire. Four of them, because they did not believe [in Christ], were tortured and burnt alive. The others, who asked for mercy, were suffocated and then burnt.

And, before they were judged, one of them (it was said to be Juan Franco) was taken to show [the inquisitors] the place where they had buried the innocent child, and they dug in the place where he was buried. And until today his body has never been found, nothing of his, not a bone, nor the shoes or hose with which he was buried. Neither was anything found except the empty tomb of the size in which they had made it, and no more. This was a mysterious thing, that nothing of that holy child has ever appeared up to today, not even the heart which the Jew took to Avila, which went wrapped in some very bloodstained cloths. Only the cloths were found, but without any blood. And thus it may be piously believed that Our Lord mysteriously wished that nothing of [the child] should remain or appear, but that he should go in bone and flesh to enjoy His holy glory in paradise. In addition to the above, it happened that, at this time, many sows which entered those caves or chambers [near La Guardia] died.

When the identity of the holy, innocent child had been discovered, they went to Toledo to look for his mother, and they found her, able to see. And she described how she had lost her son at that time and on that day, and how she was blind from birth, and on that day she had been able to see, and she did not know how it had happened. And [the inquisitors] found it to be true that, at the same day and hour that the holy child had expired, she had recovered her sight. And in this she represented Longinus, who lived with the blood and water from the side of Our Lord [having pierced it with a lance], in the same way this woman with the martyrdom and death of her son.

When, as has been said, the aforementioned Jews were imprisoned by the Holy Inquisition, a trial was undertaken against each one of them. And they were given their sentences, according to the penalty that they deserved for having done and committed so great an offence and cruelty, for which reason the trials were later moved and split, because the Avila Inquisition moved to Toledo, and the scribes and secretaries moved too, some to Valladolid and others to Granada. For this reason, it is believed that the [records of] the trials are split up, but not lost. And because it was right and just that the gentlemen [señores] who rule the council of the aforementioned town of La Guardia should have a document or memorial of how it all happened, because there was good reason that those living, and their sons, grandsons and descendants, should know of this most certain cruelty, they decided to appeal to the very reverend lord, Don Alonso de Fonseca, formerly archbishop of Toledo, to whom the aforesaid town of La Guardia belonged, in the year 1533, that he should have a copy made for them in public form. He attempted to do so in Granada, and was told that it could not be done, because it would cause confusion and passion among the inhabitants of the aforesaid town of La Guardia, and to avoid passions [*sic*] with some descendants of Jews, of whom there are many today, in the aforesaid town. Thus, as he was unable to obtain the aforementioned trials, of which there were eleven, one for each individual, a certain Rodrigo de Campuzano, citizen and native of this aforesaid town of La Guardia, made a search for the said trials, and he was told that he would find what he was looking for in the house of a certain scribe in Valladolid. And when he went there and searched diligently, he found the trial which was undertaken against Benito García Cardador, or De las Mesuras. And, as I said, he was the one who put the crown of thorns on the holy innocent child. When the aforesaid Rodrigo de Campuzano, who was present, saw this trial, he urgently requested the scribe to give him a copy of it, [for which] he would be well paid. And thus the scribe, seeing the good desire of the said Rodrigo de Campuzano, had a copy made. He gave it to him and [Rodrigo] brought it back to this town.

V: Jews in the Reformation

This may well appear to many to be the most conventional and least unexpected section of the present work, in that there is generally an unconscious or else admitted assumption that, as the Reformation changed so many things for Europe's Christians, it must therefore have had a similar effect on Jews. As a prelude to the all too familiar works of Martin Luther on the subject of the Jews, which, like those of Jean Calvin, were all based on the assumption that the only proper and logical thing for a Jew to do was to convert to Christianity, some documents are included which refer to the career and work of the German Hebraist Johann Reuchlin. Erasmus' defence of Reuchlin as a scholar is counterbalanced by the latter's own assessment of his work and its purpose, which seem to be firmly rooted in the Christian teachings and attitudes of previous centuries. It is clear that, even in the Christian Renaissance, the accurate study of the Hebrew scriptures was still regarded with suspicion, even by apparently 'enlightened' scholars. More interesting, perhaps, are Reuchlin's comments on the mystical Jewish Kabbalah, which turn late medieval Christian approaches to rabbinical Judaism in another direction, towards works which had previously hardly been considered by Christian scholars. Reuchlin's work was condemned by Christian intellectuals at the time, but the notion of Christian Hebraism was to survive through the period of the Reformation and beyond. As was indicated in chapter I [for example in document 7] the Counter-Reformation brought no positive change in Catholic attitudes towards Jews.

40. A Christian Hebraist: Johann Reuchlin

(a) Praise of the German scholar's work of Biblical translation in a prayer by the humanist Desiderius Erasmus of Rotterdam

[From 'Apotheosis of that incomparable worthy, John Reuchlin', in *The Colloquies of Erasmus;* in Latin, trans. C. R. Thompson, Chicago, 1965, p. 86]

O God, thou lover of mankind, who through thy chosen servant John Reuchlin has renewed to the world the gift of tongues, by which thou didst once from heaven, through thy Holy Spirit, instruct the apostles for the preaching of the gospel, grant that all men everywhere may preach in every tongue the glory of thy son Jesus. Confound the tongues of false apostles who band themselves [together] to build an impious tower for **Babel**, attempting to obscure thy glory whilst minded to exalt their own; since to thee alone, with Jesus thy Son our Lord, and the Holy Spirit, belongs all glory for ever and ever. Amen.

(b) Erasmus urges Reuchlin's scholarly cause in a letter, written in 1515 to Cardinal Riario at the Papal Curia in Rome.

[From *Collected works of Erasmus*, vol. 3, Toronto, 1976, letter 333, pp. 90-1; in Latin]

One thing I had almost forgotten. I beg and beseech you earnestly, in the name of those humane studies of which your Eminence has always been an outstanding patron, that that excellent man Doctor Johann Reuchlin should find you fair-minded and friendly in his business. At one stroke you will render a great service to literature and all literary men, for the greater their learning the greater their enthusiasm for him. He has all Germany in his debt, where he was the first to awake the study of Greek and Hebrew. He is a man with an exceptional knowledge of the languages, accomplished in many subjects, eminent and well-known throughout Christendom for his public works... The time had come when for his part he deserved to enjoy at his time of life a pleasant harvest from his honourable exertions, and we on our part looked to see him bring out the results of so many years' work for the common good. And so it seems outrageous to all men of good feeling, not Germans only but English and French as well, to whom he is well known through his letters, that a man of such distinction and such outstanding gifts should be persecuted with such unpleasant litigation... Believe me, whoever restores Johann Reuchlin to the arts and letters will win countless men's grateful devotion.

(c) Reuchlin's own purpose towards the Jews and in his study of Hebrew and the Kabbalah

[From *Johann Reuchlins Briefwechsel*, ed. L. Geiger, Stuttgart, 1875, letter 215, p. 245; in Latin, translated in Lloyd Jones' introduction to Reuchlin's *On the art of the Kabbalah*, p. 15]

I have suffered innocently for many years because of my very great wish to strengthen the orthodox [Catholic] faith and my most ardent desire to enlarge the Catholic Church, because I felt that those who were outside the faith, the Jews, [Orthodox] Greeks and Saracens would not be attracted to us by insults. For I considered it unbecoming of the Church to drive them to holy baptism by tyranny or severity.

(d) From Reuchlin's *De arte cabalistica* [*On the art of the Kabbalah*] dedicated to Pope Leo X and licensed for printing by Thomas Anselm, in a command of the Emperor Maximilian, issued on 21 August 1516. The book takes the form of a supposed conversation in Frankfurt-am-Main, between a Jew named Simon, with knowledge of the science of the **Kabbalah**, and two visitors, one a representative of Greek philosophy, a 'Pythagorean' called Philolaus, and the other a Muslim called Marranus (ironically, perhaps, the name used in Spain for supposedly false converts from Judaism to Christianity, which was *marrano*); in this extract Simon expounds the nature and importance of the Kabbalah.

[in Latin, trans. Martin and Sarah Goodman, New York, 1983, p. 61]

Information transmitted from the senses to the intellect is acquired by persistent study and careful reasoning, but what is transferred from the intellect to the mind, to the light of the mind, takes on the character of the divine; there is no human form with which to clothe it. No thoughts are more profound than these ... my friends, in regard for you, I have, through our studies together, imposed on you an awe-inspiring obligation. From remarks I have made in passing, you will see that Kabbalah is a study heaven-bestowed and of the utmost importance to man. Without it none can achieve something as elusive, as difficult, as the apprehension of the divine. For it is certainly not matter given to the proofs of mere mortal reasoning, empty-worded thorny arguments, man's syllogisms: the subject matter is divine; so big, so great, so infinite is it that in one generation even the tireless work of one man could not master it – even if our lifespan stretched to many generations – since we are obviously living in this mud and clay of the thick lump that is a living body, and we use the bodily senses in all we take on. The Hebrew sages say: 'Explain the power behind the work of Creation – impossible'... Metaphysics makes use of the conjectures of the natural sciences. Every higher science rightly takes for granted the conclusions of the more basic forms of knowledge and makes no attempt to demonstrate what is already proved. Assertions are unreservedly trusted, otherwise no man could in one lifetime fully investigate the smallest chain of reasoning in any one discipline. If this is what happens in human sciences, where men accept cheap, mechanical tradesmen's stuff by word of mouth, and trust those they think are good on one subject alone, then are we to despise the tradition ['handing down' – hence 'Kabbalah' in the Hebrew] of these holy men, in accepting this knowledge of the divine, where none of us is really able to approach the subject?

Kabbalah is a matter of divine revelation handed down to further the contemplation of the distinct Forms and of God, contemplation bringing salvation; Kabbalah is the receiving of this through symbols.

(e) Reuchlin's own defence of his Hebrew grammar and dictionary, *De rudimentis hebraicis*, Pforzheim, 1506, reprinted 1974

[Reproduced in the introduction by Gareth Lloyd Jones to Johann Reuchlin, *On the art of the Kabbalah*, trans. Martin and Sarah Goodman, New York, 1983, p. 13]

I believe that [Christian] enemies will oppose our dictionary, in which the interpretations of many are frequently criticized. What a crime!', they will exclaim. 'Nothing is more unworthy of the memory of the [Church] fathers, no crime more cruel, than the attempt made by that most audacious man to overthrow so many and such saintly men who were imbued with the Holy Spirit. The Bible of the most blessed Jerome [the Vulgate] was accepted in the Church, as Pope Gelasius testifies. The venerable father Nicholas of Lyra, the common expositor of the Bible, is considered by all who are faithful to Christ to be the soundest of men. Now a certain puff of smoke has appeared who claims that these have translated erroneously in a great many places.' To such threatening shouts I reply with these few words: 'Allow me what was allowed to those famous luminaries'.

41. Martin Luther on the Jews

(a) *That Jesus Christ was born a Jew*. Luther attempts to refute the accusation, debated in the Diet of Nuremberg in 1522 and elsewhere in Germany, that he rejected the 'virgin birth' of Jesus and regarded Joseph as the Christian saviour's natural father. When this text was composed in 1523, Martin Luther was primarily interested in the reform of the Catholic Church and regarded the Papacy as his main enemy.

[From *Luther's works*, vol. 45, ed. Walther I. Brandt, Philadelphia, 1962, pp. 199-229; in German]

A new lie about me is being circulated. I am supposed to have preached and written that Mary, the mother of God, was not a virgin either before or after the birth of Christ, but that she conceived Christ through Joseph, and had more children after that. Above and beyond all this, I am supposed to have preached a new heresy, namely, that Christ was [through Joseph] the seed of Abraham. How these lies tickle my good friends the papists!...

Since for the sake of others, however, I am compelled to answer these lies, I thought I would also write something useful in addition, so that I do not vainly steal the reader's time with such dirty rotten business. Therefore I will cite from Scripture the reasons that move me to believe that Christ was a Jew born of a virgin, that I might perhaps also win some Jews to the Christian faith. Our fools, the popes, bishops, sophists [scholastic theologians], and monks — the crude asses' heads — have hitherto so treated the Jews that anyone who wished to become a good Christian would almost have had to become a Jew. If I had been a Jew and had seen such dolts and blockheads govern and teach the Christian faith, I would sooner have become a hog than a Christian.

They have dealt with the Jews as if they were dogs rather than human beings; they have done little else but deride them and seize their property. When they baptize them they show them nothing of Christian doctrine or life, but only subject them to popishness and monkery. When the Jews then see that Judaism has such strong support in Scripture, and that Christianity has become a mere babble without reliance on Scripture, how can they possibly compose themselves and become right good Christians? I have myself heard from pious baptized Jews that if they had not in our day heard the gospel they would have remained Jews under the cloak of Christianity for the rest of their days. For they acknowledge that they have never yet heard anything about Christ from those who baptized and taught them.

I hope that if one deals in a kindly way with the Jews and instructs them carefully from Holy Scripture, many of them will become genuine Christians and turn again to the faith of their fathers, the prophets and patriarchs. They will only be frightened further away from it if their Judaism is so utterly rejected that nothing is allowed to remain, and they are treated with arrogance and scorn. If the apostles, who were also Jews, had dealt with us Gentiles as we Gentiles deal with the Jews, there would never have been a Christian among the Gentiles. Since they dealt with us Gentiles in such brotherly fashion, we in turn ought to treat the Jews in a brotherly manner, in order that we might convert some of them. For even we ourselves are not yet all very far along [the Christian way], not to speak of having arrived.

When we are inclined to boast of our position we should remember that we are but Gentiles, while the Jews are of the lineage of Christ. We are aliens and in-laws; they are blood-relatives, cousins and brothers of Our Lord. Therefore, if one is to boast of flesh and blood, the Jews are actually nearer to Christ than we are, as St Paul says in Romans 9 [:5]. God has also demonstrated this by his acts, for to no nation among the Gentiles has he granted so high an honour as he has to the Jews. For from among the Gentiles there have been raised up no patriarchs, no apostles, no prophets, indeed very few Christians either. And although the gospel has been proclaimed to all the world, yet He committed the Holy Scriptures, that is the Law and the prophets, to no nation except the Jews....

If the Jews should take offence because we confess our Jesus to be a man, and yet true God, we will deal forcefully with that from Scripture in due time. But this is too harsh for a beginning. Let them first be suckled with milk and begin by recognizing this man Jesus as the true Messiah; after that they may drink wine, and learn also that he is true God. For they have been led astray so long and so far that one must deal gently with them, as people who have been all too strongly indoctrinated to believe that God cannot be man.

Therefore, I would request and advise that one deal gently with them and instruct them from Scripture; then some of them may come along. Instead of this we are trying only to drive them by force, slandering them, accusing them of having Christian blood if they don't stink [*sic*], and I know not what other foolishness. So long as we treat them thus like dogs, how can we expect to work any good among them? Again, when we forbid them to labour and do business and have any human fellowship with us, thereby forcing them into usury, how is that supposed to do them any good?

If we really want to help them, we must be guided in our dealings with them not by papal law but by the law of Christian love. We must receive them cordially, and permit them to trade and work with us, that they may have occasion and opportunity to associate with us, hear our Christian teaching, and witness our Christian life. If some of them should prove stiff-necked, what of it? After all, we ourselves are not all good Christians either.

(b) *On the Jews and their lies*: Luther's later view of the Jews, from the year 1543

[From: *Luther's works*, vol. 47, ed. Franklin Sherman, Philadelphia, 1971, pp. 137-306; in German]

[p. 137] I had made up my mind to write no more either about the Jews or against them. But since I learned that these miserable and accursed people do not cease to lure to themselves even us, that is the Christians, I have published this little book, so that I might be found among those who opposed such poisonous activities of the Jews and who warned the Christians to be on their guard against them. I would not have believed that a Christian could be duped by the Jews into taking their exile and wretchedness upon himself. However, the devil is the god of the world, and wherever God's word is absent he has an easy task, not only with the weak but also with the strong. May God help us. Amen....

[pp. 137, 139] It is not my purpose to quarrel with the Jews, nor to learn from them how they interpret or understand Scripture; I know all of that very well already. Much less do I propose to convert the Jews, for that is impossible... In short, ... do not engage much in debate with Jews about the articles of our faith. From their youth they have been so nurtured with venom and rancour against our Lord that there is no hope until they reach the point where their misery finally makes them pliable and they are forced to confess that the Messiah has come, and that he is our Jesus.

[p. 140] ... In comparison with them, and in their eyes, we Gentiles [Goyim] are not human; in fact we hardly deserve to be considered poor worms by them. For we are not of that high and noble blood, lineage, birth and descent. This is their argument, and indeed I think it is the greatest and strongest reason for their pride and boasting.

Therefore God has to endure that in their synagogues, their prayers, songs, doctrines and their whole life, they come and stand before him and plague him grievously (if I may speak of God in such a human fashion).

[p. 290] Neither Jew nor devil will in any way be able to prove that our belief that the one eternal Godhead is composed of three persons implies that we believe in more than one God. If the Jews maintain that they cannot understand how three persons can be one god, why then must their blasphemous, accursed, lying mouth deny, condemn and curse what it does not understand?....

[p. 292] I wish and I ask that our rulers who have Jewish subjects exercise a sharp mercy towards these wretched people, as suggested above, to see whether this might not help (though this is doubtful). They must act like a good physician who, when gangrene has set in, proceeds without mercy to cut, saw and burn flesh, veins, bone and marrow. Such a procedure must also be followed in this instance. Burn down their synagogues, forbid all that I enumerated earlier, force them to work and deal harshly with them, as Moses did in the wilderness, slaying three thousand lest the whole people perish. They surely do not know what they are doing; moreover, as people possessed, they do not wish to know it, hear it or learn it. Therefore it would be wrong to be merciful and confirm them in their conduct. If this does not help we must drive them out like mad dogs, so that we do not become partakers of their abominable blasphemy and all the other vices and thus merit God's wrath and be damned with them. I have done my duty. Now let everyone see to his. I am exonerated.

42. Jean Calvin on the Jews

Text on the Jews composed in 1560

[From: Jean Calvin, *Institution de la Religion Chrestienne*, ed. Jean-Daniel Benoît, Paris, 1957, book 2; in French]

(a) The Law and the prophets superseded by Christianity

[Chapter 9, pp. 189-90]

Since God did not institute in former times the sacrifices and purgations [of the Jewish Law] in order to give a frustrating witness to the Jews, since he was their Father, [and] seeing that he did not dedicate them to Himself in vain as a Chosen people, there is no doubt that He made Himself known to them in the same image in which He appears to us today with full clarity. Because [the prophet] Malachi, after having urged the Jews to pay attention to the Law of Moses, and to follow it constantly (because straight after [Malachi's] death there was to be an interruption in the course of the prophecies), he says that if they do not fail at all in this, the Sun of Righteousness will be sent to them, and will rise soon [Malachi 4:2]. By this he indicates that the usage of the [Mosaic] Law was intended to support them in waiting for Christ, whose coming was imminent. However, greater clarity was to be expected from Him. For this reason, Saint Peter says that the prophets searched carefully for and made enquiry after the salvation which is today shown to us in the Gospel; and that it was revealed to them that they were not working so much for themselves and their age as for us, when they administered the secrets which are today announced to us by the Gospel [1 Peter 1:10-12]. Not that their teaching was without use to the ancient people [of the Jews], nor did they fail to profit from it themselves, but they heard nothing of the treasure [Christ], whom God sent us by their hand. For in our day, the grace of which they were [once] witnesses has been sent specially to us, before their very eyes, and whereas they had a small taste of it, we have it in much greater abundance. Even though Christ says that he was witnessed to by Moses [John 5:46], he does not cease to emphasise how far we [Christians] surpass the Jews; for, when speaking to his disciples, 'Blessed', he said, 'are the eyes which see what you see, and the ears which hear what you hear. Many kings and prophets desired this and did not obtain it' [Matthew 13:16-17; Luke 10: 23-24].

(b) God's promise to the Jews

[Chapter 6, pp. 112-13]

Now God has willed that the Jews should be filled with such prophecies in order to accustom them to direct their eyes to Jesus Christ, provided and inasmuch as they had to ask to be saved. And in fact, however much they have been wickedly bastardized, it has not been possible for the memory of this principle to be abolished: that is, that God, according to his promise to [King] David, would be the redeemer of his church by the hand of Jesus Christ. And that by this means, the free covenant, by which God had adopted his chosen ones, would be firm. It was because of this that it came about that, at Christ's entry into Jerusalem shortly before his death, this song rang out as a commonplace in the mouths of the little children: 'Hosannah to the Son of David!' [Matthew 21:9]. For there is no doubt at all that [this chant] was not taken from what was generally received among the whole people, and that they did not sing it every day. That is to say, there remained to them no other pledge of God's mercy than the coming of the Redeemer. For this reason, Christ commands his disciples to believe in him, so that they may believe distinctly and perfectly in God [John 14:1].... Now, however much the Scribes [of the Jewish Law] may have, by their false commentaries, blurred and obscured everything that the Prophets had taught concerning the Redeemer, Jesus Christ took this article [of faith] to be agreed and received by common consent: that is, that there was no other remedy for the confusion into which the Jews had fallen, nor any other means of delivering the Church, than that the promised redeemer should come first. What Saint Paul teaches has not been as well understood among the people as it was required to be, that is to say that Jesus Christ is the completion of the [Jewish] Law [Romans 10:4].

(c) That the Law was given, not to restrict the Ancient People [the Jews] to themselves, but to nourish the hope of salvation that it was to have in Jesus Christ, until he came

[title of Chapter 7, p. 115]

From all the discourse that we have made, it is easy to gather that the

Law was not given, about four hundred years after the death of Abraham, in order to distance the chosen people from Jesus Christ, but rather to keep their spirits in suspense until his advent, and to incite them to an ardent desire for that coming, also to confirm them during the wait, so that they should not weaken because of the length of time. Now, by this term 'the Law', I do not only understand the ten commandments, which show us the rule of living justly and in a holy manner, but the [whole] form of religion as God announced it by the hand of Moses. For Moses was not given as a Law-maker in order to abolish the blessing promised to Abraham's race; rather, we see that in various places [ça et là] he recalls the Israelites to this free covenant, that God had established with their fathers and of which they were heirs, as if he had been sent to renew it. Which has been amply demonstrated by the ceremonies [of the Law]. For there would be nothing more stupid and frivolous than to offer the fat and stinking smoke of the entrails of animals in order to be reconciled with God, or to have as one's refuge some pouring out of blood or water in order to clean the stains of the soul. In short, if all the service which there has been under the Law is considered for its own sake, as if it contained no shadows or figures which had their corresponding [Christian] truths, it will seem that it is a game for little children.

VI: Jews in European culture

If earlier sections of this book appear to have been put together at random (even though they have not), this must particularly seem to be the case when it comes to the matter of Jewish culture. In some circles, it is still a matter of dispute whether there is such a thing as Jewish culture at all. The question is whether Jewish intellectual and cultural activity in a non-Jewish context may be included under such a heading.

This chapter has been compiled on the basis that it can. Thus extracts from the authentic Jewish preaching of the period, in Spain and Italy, are set alongside papal attempts to protect, for reasons described in the relevant texts, the continuance of rabbinical scholarship in early sixteenth-century Italy. Apart from one case of a Jewish alchemist in Germany, the rest of the documents in this chapter originated in Italy. They show everyday interaction between Jews and Christians (and, in the case of document 48, Spanish converts from Judaism as well), in such disparate areas as the disposal of Christian art-works in a house newly owned by Jews, and Jewish contributions to the famous Roman Carnival. The chapter concludes with extracts from the autobiography of Leon Modena, one of the greatest of all Italian Jewish scholars, who, though hardly, in one sense, a 'typical' individual himself, nonetheless succeeds in conveying an extraordinary number of vivid impressions of the good and bad features of Jewish life in Italy at the end of the sixteenth century.

In view of the history of Jewish residence in a variety of western European countries, it was inevitable that Jews would acquire a wide range of linguistic skills. Nonetheless, it is undeniable that there was a tendency for Jewish communities to take on the cultural characteristics of the countries in which they lived. This was particularly true of the Iberian [Spanish and Portuguese, or 'Sephardic'] Jews who took their languages into exile after 1492 and 1497 respectively, thus creating what is today known as Ladino, and northern European ['Ashkenazi'] Jews who gave the world the Yiddish language, based on medieval German. The scene was thus set for the development of Jewish life in western, as well as central and eastern Europe in the years after 1600.

43. Jewish preaching: Spain and Italy

[From Marc Saperstein, *Jewish preaching, 1200-1800. An anthology*, New Haven and London, 1989, English translation from Hebrew]

(a) A late-fifteenth century comparison of Jewish and Christian preaching in Spain, by Isaac Arama, in his introduction to *Agudat Yitzhak*, in Saperstein, pp. 392-3.

These Jews among whom I lived [in Tarragona] loved God's Torah deeply. They desired nothing so much as to listen to its words with exegetical and homiletical commentary, to understand interpretations both ancient and new, to search for reasonable explanations of problematic passages. This is what they looked forward to day and night, on each festival and Sabbath.

I set myself to satisfy this desire from the works of the great masters of the past, who have illumined our path with their interpretations. But I was unable to fill the needs of the people as expressed to me by their questions. For our Jews are an intellectual people [*am binot*], and they dwell in the midst of another people with profound and articulate speakers everywhere: the refined people of Edom. In every city, their scholars master all branches of knowledge, their priests and princes stand at the fore in philosophy, integrating it with their theological doctrine. They have written many books, on the basis of which biblical texts are expounded before large congregations. Each day their preachers give important insights into their religion and faith, thereby sustaining it.

For some time now, calls have gone out far and wide, summoning the people to hear their learned discourses. They have fulfilled their promise. Among those who came were Jews. They heard the preachers and found them impressive; their appetites were whetted for similar fare. This is what they say: 'The Christian scholars and sages raise questions and seek answers in their academies and churches, thereby adding to the glory of the Torah and the prophets, as do the sages of every people. Why should the divine Torah, with all its narratives and pronouncements, be as a veiled maiden beside the flocks of her friends and her students?'

The Gentiles search enthusiastically for religious and ethical content, using all appropriate hermeneutical techniques, even the thirteen rules for interpreting the Torah, including the argument a *fortiori* and the verbal analogy. But our Torah commentators do not employ this method that everyone admires. Their purpose is only to explain the grammatical forms of words and the simple meaning of the stories and commandments. They have not attempted to fill our need or to exalt the image of our Torah to our own people by regaling them with gems from its narratives and laws.

(b) A sermon by Joseph ibn Shem Tob, preached in Segovia on the third sabbath after Passover 1452.

[From Saperstein, pp. 169-71, 179; in Hebrew]

In the year 5212 [1452] of the world's creation, when Prince Henry [later Henry IV of Castile], may God bless him, had come to the cities of Andalusia, the community of Segovia sent to him two distinguished Jews. Their mission concerned those who had risen against them and spread evil libels on the day of the hanging of their messiah [Good Friday] in order to plunder and despoil. He commanded me to go to the people giving me letters to the governor [of the castle] and the leaders of the city and a document of good faith for the Jewish community, bringing them solace and reassurance.

I arrived in [Segovia] on Friday, exhausted from the long journey. I was also emotionally wrought up. I stood trembling and berated the nobles and city notables for not having intervened against their enemies [and ours]. Early the next morning, the entire [Jewish community] gathered in the Great Synagogue. After the reading of the Torah, I stood up and began to speak. This is what I said: 'All is foreseen, and free will is given' [Abot 3:15, a Talmudic text]...

[Rabbi Aqiba] compares the status of rebels and sinners, or indeed of society as a whole, to a pharmacy and its owner. There in his pharmacy, he mixes from various kinds of powder the simple and complex drugs, including poisons and antidotes. All can be cured through his work. The pharmacist is a good and gentle man, concerned about the welfare of his city. When people want something, he gives them what they request, whether it be food or medicines or drugs, but it goes on their account, and they must pay him the true value.

This pharmacist has considerable power in the city. His net is spread over its inhabitants so that no-one can flee owing him money for what has been taken. The store is open day and night, and the inhabitants of the city can easily obtain whatever they need from it, but the pharmacist watches carefully to see what everyone decides to take. As a wise man who tries to ensure that he will be paid what is owed him, he writes down in his record book all that he gives out. 'The account book is open, and the hand of the scribe is writing'....

Now although this shop contains some dangerous things – including poisons – the drugs are actually extremely beneficial. However, an ignorant person who does not know their beneficial properties may be harmed by them. For example, syrup of anacardium [oriental cashew] can be fatal, yet if properly prepared and administered it can help with weakness of mind or forgetfulness. Someone who takes it for pleasure may hallucinate, but there is no problem when it is used properly. 'All is prepared for the banquet'.

This marvellous image refers to important issues concerning the equity of God's actions. The 'Judge of the entire world' [Genesis 18:25] has given human beings free will and empowered them to eat 'from all the trees in the garden' [Genesis 2:16], to make use of all things placed in this world as they choose. These things are good when used in the proper place and in proper measure. One might say that even the impulse towards evil is good, for without it we would not be able to have children. This is what Rabbi Meir said in Genesis Rabbah, 'Dying is good'.

This passage explains that things thought to be fundamentally evil are actually fundamentally good when properly used. Some are good because of their effect. An example would be punishments that cleanse the soul and turn it in the proper direction. That is what is meant in the statement, 'This is Hell'. And some are good because of what necessarily follows them. An example would be death, which is necessarily followed by a different mode of being....

[Finally, Joseph directly refers to the anti-Jewish attacks in Segovia which had caused him to go to Andalusia to see the lord of the town, Prince Henry.]

He is a fool who says that had it not been for that incident [the crucifixion of Jesus], those murders and conflagrations and forced apostasies would never have befallen our sacred communities. Nothing prevents God from fabricating new causes and different libels to be directed against us as justification for the collection of His debt. 'He has a basis of support.' Look at the Jewish communities in Islamic lands. Murders and forced apostasies have befallen them without any libels relating to the death of that man [Jesus].

Instead, we should look into our behaviour, as individuals and as a community. This is why these tragedies occur. They are brought by the collectors who make their rounds each day to collect the debts. The situation can be remedied only by removing the cause. It is a foolish physician who concentrates exclusively on treating the illness and its symptoms without removing the underlying cause....

Now making requests of kings and entreating the great nobles, all of whom are direct and immediate causes of events, is an appropriate human endeavour. But it is not a fundamental remedy. The essential, underlying cause is our transgressions. This will lead to the cure of the disease itself. Once this is remedied, all else will be, for 'The mind of the king is in the hand of God' [Proverbs 21:1]. In particular, what must be remedied is the abuse of bans of excommunication, acts of informing to the authorities, the eating of forbidden foods and the drinking of Gentile wine, in which matters very many have stumbled. 'Great is the Lord and full of power' [Psalm 147:5]. He has already seen that our people have done evil, and he has permitted them [the Christians] to chastise us for our sins. 'All is foreseen, and free will is given.'

(c) Sermon on the relationship between Jewish and non-Jewish scholarship, preached by Judah Moscato, Mantua, c. 1585: Sermon for the second day of the feast of Weeks.

[From Saperstein, pp. 255-7, 268-9, in Hebrew]

Yesterday we began to reveal the great and powerful benefit attainable in no other way than through devotion to the Torah. Let us now pass to a theoretical investigation of this matter, to be taken as far as the subject allows, and then supplement it with hidden content of mighty statements from the rabbis and the Bible.

Reason and logic make it clear to all that nourishment must befit the nature of that which is to be nourished. Now just as this is true for the body and its physical nourishment, so it is true for the rational soul: it is nourished and sustained by that which characteristically pertains to the intellect alone. But the rational soul is derived from the realm of supernal and eternal beings. Just as they are nourished and sustained in life with nourishment befitting their nature by the rational apprehension of their creator, so the rational soul must receive its nourishment and life-giving sustenance from this same source. None other will do.

As we now search through the various philosophical disciplines, the correctness of my premise will be established. Do you not see that the propaedeutic disciplines cannot possibly serve as nourishment befitting the vital sustenance of the rational soul? Their subject matter depends entirely on things conceived by the intellect that have no reality outside the mind, things that are intellectually abstracted from matter, both ontologically and categorically. In this sense they do not really exist. Nor can the natural sciences [nourish the rational soul], for their subject matter is constantly changing.

Nor can that which is called in philosophy 'the divine science', that is, metaphysics, for theoretical investigation in this realm is merely wild speculation and surmise fraught with doubt, as its practitioners themselves concede. Further proof of this is the variety of incompatible views on basic questions. And even that which they are able to apprehend through their rational investigation is but 'base silver laid over earthenware' [Proverbs 26:23], for although they acknowledge the existence of a 'First Cause', they have 'ardent lips with an evil mind' [*ibid.*] in associating the Name of God with something totally different, from which, as they assert, everything results by necessity. In short, all of the disciplines of human learning are inadequate as sources of vital sustenance for the rational soul.

This is not true of the divine Torah. Its subject matter is the creation of the world, the wondrous works of the One who is perfect in knowledge: pure intelligible ideas, capable of fully satisfying the rational soul with appropriate nourishment. Thus the benefit to be derived from the Torah, great and powerful, is unattainable from any other source. This is the meaning of the verse, 'For man does not live by bread alone, but by all that issues from the mouth of the Lord' [Deuteronomy 8:3]. As the human being is composed of body and soul, there must be a special kind of nourishment for each part. Bread, composed of the [physical] elements, befits the body, which is also composed of them. But 'that which issues from the mouth of the Lord' befits the rational part, for God has made one correspond to the other for our perpetual good ....

Now you may ask, why did the sages [Talmudic rabbis] speak of ethical and philosophical matters by way of allegories and enigmas ...? After all, the contents of their teachings are not one of the secret doctrines of the Torah, which we are commanded to conceal. On the contrary, the *aggadah* includes important principles that should be engraved on the tablets of our hearts. Why then did they not teach them explicitly?

I will answer after noting that the rabbis themselves addressed this issue in several ways. One was, 'When they became weary of technical legal study, they engaged in words of jest'; another explanation was that this was a way of sharpening their minds. However, I will also say my own piece in answer to this question. The sages, recognising the value and importance of the matters to which they alluded, wanted to make a powerful impression. Now it is clear that people hold in greatest esteem that which they must expend their effort to obtain.

Proof of this is to be found in children. What is highly esteemed will always be remembered. Furthermore, the effort itself causes the subject to be remembered, as the sages have said, 'The wisdom I acquired in anger [has remained with me]'.

This is why the sages decided to incorporate these precious teachings, so beneficial to others, in statements that are obscure in their language, knowing that these teachings would remain in the shadows until the true wisdom of their words was discovered by the wise luminaries among the people. As they plumb the full depth of the sages' teachings, after the effort and toil of their investigation, they will love and esteem what they have discovered. These doctrines will be fully impressed upon their thought, and they will benefit, even if this was not their original intent. Others, too, who hear these statements explained by those who have uncovered their true meaning, will derive benefit from the joy and pleasure which they feel in finally understanding after they have been entangled in the realm of allegory and enigma.

In summary, we have found that disciplines other than the divine Torah cannot adequately measure or define that which pertains either to the intellect or to the realm of action. God's Torah, which is perfect, can do both. These are the wings which enable us to ascend to the heights of heaven and find shelter under the wings of the One who is to be blessed, praised and glorified for his bounteous love and goodness. Let us sing to him in joy, 'How precious is your loving kindness, God! Human beings take refuge in the shadow of your wings'.

44. Rabbinical scholarship protected by the pope: Italy, 1519, 1530

(a) Bologna, 1519: the bishop of Ostia, chamberlain to Pope Leo X, grants various privileges to Abraham Cohen, rabbi of the Bologna community, for ten years, including a licence to travel without paying duty on his books, and not having to wear the Jewish badge. Dated at Rome, 10 August 1519.

[From Simonsohn, *Documents: 1464–1521*, no. 1272, pp. 1593-5; in Latin]

Raphael, by the divine mercy bishop of Ostia, cardinal of St George, chamberlain of our most holy lord the pope and of the Holy Roman Church, to Master Abraham, formerly Moses, a Spanish Jew, priest [*sic*] and doctor of the Jewish Law, inhabitant of the city of Bologna, [who is] ignorant of the way of truth and how to keep it.

Desiring to reduce you to the cult of the Catholic faith, a thing which we are sure you will do even more willingly when you have found us to be so much more well-intentioned towards you and your family's good, we have heard from you that you have great familiarity and conversation with great Christian men, scholars of ecclesiastical matters and of the Christian faith and the law of the Gospel, who receive not inconsiderable help in their studies from your learning. As a result of this, it happens that you accept their summons, whether in due course or immediately, to various places [under the jurisdiction] of the Holy Roman Church. They make you carry and transport your Hebrew and also your Latin books, not without great expense, above all in customs dues [*gabellæ*], so that you have acted to appeal to us humbly that we may deign to make provision for you in this matter as is appropriate.

We, accepting your supplications in these matters, by order of our most holy lord the pope, given to us orally in this matter, and by the authority of our office as chamberlain, authorise you to go to whatever place in the Papal states you are required to visit, in whatever way, with all your books, and especially the Hebrew ones, whether manuscript or printed, for your use, study and exercise, without any payment of taxes or duties. Also, by these presents we concede and graciously grant, for as long as this our concession may last, that you and your wife, and your children, whether already born or yet to be born, with all your family and household, may, go, be present, dwell, act and converse, go away or return, absolutely as you please and as is appropriate for you, without the note and sign of the letter 'O' [the Jewish badge], and without a [Jewish] hat or veils, respectively, for your wife and household, whether in yellow or any other colour, and similarly with any other badge for male or female Jews which may be ordered in any other place in the apostolic decrees, laws or statutes.

[It is made clear in the rest of the document that such concessions were not to be extended to other rabbis in the Papal states.]

(b) Rome, 1530: Pope Clement VII grants an indulgence to Rabbi Salamon Molcho, a Portuguese Jew who had been forcibly baptised in his youth, to publish some books concerning Holy Scripture, provided that they were first examined by the master of the papal palace and found to contain nothing contrary to Catholic teaching. Dated at Rome, 20 May 1530.

[From Simonsohn, *Documents: 1522-1538*, pp. 1792-3; in Latin]

To Rabbi Salamon, a Portuguese Jew, ignorant of the way of truth, [in the hope] that you will be brought to salvation. Seeing that, as you have recently made known to us, you unwillingly underwent the sacrament of baptism while still a boy, and have never believed in the Catholic faith, and have never lived under any other than the Jewish Law, nor intend to do so, We, being aware that it is fitting for the Apostolic See, out of its wish to bring the Jews to its bosom by kindness, as they are specially preserved as a witness to the orthodox faith, and wishing, in so far as is appropriate for us, to respond favourably to your requests, and being in this way inclined towards your supplications, so that you should be troubled as little as possible on account of the above by whatever authority, in the terms of these presents grant you indulgence, by our special command and apostolic authority.

And moreover, since, as we have accepted, you are having printed certain books concerning the subject of Holy Scripture, we, for the common utility of the faithful, give you full and free licence to have them printed by those who print books and practise the art of books. And [also decree] that nothing should be inserted by the printers who print these same books which goes against the truth of the Catholic faith, under the penalties of a general sentence of excommunication and the confiscation of the books printed. In particular, we thus forbid these books [to be printed] unless they have first been carefully examined by whatever beloved son of ours may currently be appointed by the master of our sacred palace in Rome.

45. The Jew as alchemist: Germany, 1472

Sixtus IV, in an order dated in Rome on 9 June 1472, permits the provost of St Mary, Flonheim, in the diocese of Mainz, to reconcile, after penance, Heinrich Foxe, a priest in the diocese of Trier, for allowing a Jewish alchemist to reside in his house. The accusation seems to be concerned more with the supposed circulation of forged coinage than with the alchemy itself.

[Simonsohn, *The Apostolic See and the Jews: Documents, 1464–1521*, pp. 1195–6; in Latin]

Sixtus, etc. To our beloved son, the provost of the church of Blessed Mary in Flanheim, in the diocese of Mainz, greetings, etc. The Apostolic See, like a merciful mother, readily shows itself to be gracious and full of good will towards its sons who, after [having committed] excess, return to it in humility. Thus, there has recently been made known to us, on behalf of Heinrich Foxe, priest of the diocese of Trier a petition which said that, when he previously moved to the town of Bornich, in the aforementioned diocese, and had his house and dwelling there, and was conducting himself decently and honourably, serving the [ecclesiastical] benefices which he had obtained there, he received into his aforesaid house a Jewish person commonly known as the master of the alchemists of Nuremberg, believing him to be of good life, conversation and fame. And [the Jew] stayed with him for some time. [The priest] supplied him with material goods and other things, but when the said alchemist, who was a Jew, was recognised by some other people, this same Heinrich expelled him from his house. Also, [the petition states] that it is alleged in some quarters that the aforesaid Jew forged false coins in the house of the aforesaid Heinrich, with which he paid this same Heinrich for the latter's expenses on his behalf and for his lodging. The said Heinrich, believing this money to be good and not forged, spent it in the acquisition of necessary goods, though not more than two or three Rhineland florins [in total].

And since the aforesaid Heinrich, who was ignorant of all the above, was informed about it, and it was said that this money was forged by him, together with the aforesaid Jew, and since the aforesaid Heinrich never offered help, advice, or favour or support to this same Jew, as is contained in his petition, the aforesaid Heinrich deeply regrets having kept the aforesaid Jew in his house and having lived with him, and having supplied him with necessaries, and having circulated the aforesaid monies, which he believed to be good.

[The priest asked, in the circumstances, to be absolved of all ecclesiastical sanctions, and Pope Sixtus granted the petition.]

46. The Jew, religion and art: Italy, 1491

The bishop of Pisa's deputy has to deal with a case in which one of the city's Jews, Isaac di Vitale, found pictures of St Christopher in his house.

[From 'Ebrei, Chiesa locale, "Principe" e Popolo: due episodi di distruzione di immagini sacre alla fine del Quattrocento', in Michele Luzzati, *La casa dell'Ebreo. Saggi sugli Ebrei a Pisa e in Toscana nel Medioevo e nel Rinascimento, Cultura e Storia Pisana*, 7, Pisa, 1985, pp. 228-34; in Italian]

(a) Isaac asks permission to remove the pictures: Pisa, 24 November 1491

Isaac di Vitale, a Jew of Pisa, appears before you, Reverend Father Master Roberto Strozzi, **vicar** of the Most Reverend lord archbishop [*sic*] of Pisa and your office and court, and reverently describes and states how, some months ago, the said Isaac, having his house, in which he normally lived, in great disorder and need of major restoration, because it was and is almost in ruins, in order to repair it and for the greater convenience, utility and necessity of himself and of his family, began to carry out and have carried out certain works and building in the aforesaid house which is his customary dwelling, situated in Pisa by the chapel of St Margaret, in order to repair the aforesaid ruinous house and in order to live in it better and more conveniently.

Also, the aforesaid Isaac describes and states how, in a certain part of the aforesaid house, namely in a most vile, rough and abject place, where people hardly go any more, and which is not used by anyone, there is a painting, or rather an image or picture, of St Christopher, and in another place in the aforesaid house, that is to say on a pillar in the hall of the first floor of the aforesaid house, another picture and image, also of St Christopher. According to the judgement and advice of the master masons, in order that they may restore and repair the said building and works, there is need and necessity that these pictures and images of St Christopher should be destroyed and removed from that place.

And in order that, by the removal and destruction of the said pictures, the aforesaid Isaac, because he is a Jew, should not or for a moment come to any harm, danger or injury, and also in order that it should not appear for a moment that the aforesaid Isaac or any of his family had removed or destroyed the said pictures in abuse and contempt of the Christian faith or of the aforesaid saint, but only by force, need and necessity, for this reason the aforesaid Isaac requests you, Master Vicar, to be pleased to grant and concede to the aforesaid Isaac and to any master mason he may call upon, that they may be able to remove and destroy the said pictures of Saint Christopher, properly and with impunity and without any harm, trouble, danger or expense to themselves. And the aforesaid Isaac outlines and demands the above in the best way that he possibly can, always recommending himself to your Reverence.

The above petition was displayed and produced before the said Lord Vicar by the said Isaac on 24 November 1492, in his tenth year of office [*indictione X*], in the Pisan style.

(b) The pictures of the saint are to be inspected

Which same lord Roberto, Vicar, having seen and heard the above, and wishing to proceed in the matter properly, correctly and legitimately, committed to, imposed on and commanded the venerable lord Bartolomeo de Morrona, canon of Pisa, that he should go in person to the house of the aforesaid Isaac, and see the place or places where the said pictures and images of the aforesaid Saint Christopher are said to be, and ascertain whether what the aforesaid Isaac described and narrated was and is true, and whether it is necessary for the said Isaac to destroy, obliterate and remove the said pictures in order to carry out his [building] works, and that he should report to the aforesaid Vicar and his court, what his own conscience told him should best be done in the above case.

(c) A report follows the inspection, both of them on the day the petition was presented

This same Lord Bartolomeo, having been there and come back, reported in person to the aforesaid lord Vicar and his court, and to me Carlo, the notary mentioned below, on the aforesaid 24th day of November, that he went to the said house of the said Isaac and saw the said house, which was and is in the greatest need of repair, because of its age and antiquity. He also reported that he saw the place or places where the images and pictures of St Christopher are, and having considered the nature of the site of one of the aforesaid images, which is wretched, and in a vile and wretched state, where no-one ever, or only rarely, passes or goes, and having seen the other place, that is, the pillar and hall in which is the other image, and having seen the building and works which the aforesaid Isaac intends to carry out and have done, he considers it necessary to destroy and remove the said images and pictures, otherwise the aforesaid Isaac will not be able to carry out his said buildings and works, or make improvements. And, having also seen that the aforesaid Isaac does not bear in his soul any calumny of or contempt for the Christian faith, but rather his own need, and having seen and considered all the other things which were to be seen and considered concerning the above, [Canon Bartolomeo] reported to the aforesaid lord Vicar and to me, Carlo, the notary mentioned below, his opinion concerning the above, which is that it would be better and more practical to grant a licence to the said Isaac to destroy the said pictures and images of Saint Christopher … because it is not proper that such figures and images should stand, be and remain in the house of Jews, and for that reason, it is better and more practical to give the said Isaac the aforementioned licence than not to do so.

(d) The holy pictures can be effaced in the course of repairs to the Jew's house

This same lord Robert, Vicar, having seen the petition of the aforesaid

Isaac, which was shown and produced before him, and having examined the commission which he gave to the said Bartolomeo de Morrona, also having examined [the canon's] report, and having seen and considered whatever had to be seen and considered in and concerning the above, gave and conceded to the aforesaid Isaac, who was present, petitioning and accepting, licence, authority and power to destroy and take away and remove the said pictures and images from the said places, and to do with them whatever he regarded as appropriate for the completion, functioning, repair and perfection of his aforesaid house, legally and without penalty and without any harm, danger, prejudice, interest or expense. The aforesaid lord Vicar also declared and affirmed that the said Isaac did not make his petition out of calumny or in contempt of the Christian faith, but only and for no other reason than his own convenience and the needs of himself and his family, and not for any other cause, and accepted the above and granted the petition, as best he could and can do under the law, in the presence of the aforesaid Isaac.

46. Jews and the Roman carnival, 1472

Mandate from Pope Sixtus IV to his officials in the Papal states, requiring Jews in their jurisdiction to contribute to the cost of the Roman carnival: this at the request of the Jewish community of Rome.

[From Simonsohn, *The Apostolic See and the Jews. Documents*, 1464–1521, no. 948, pp. 1183–4, dated at Rome, 24 January 1472, in Latin]

To Latino, by the divine mercy bishop of Tusculum, etc. Since the Jewish community [*universitas Hebreorum*] in Rome [*alma urbe*], by ancient custom and for a number of years has been required to contribute a certain sum of money towards the expenses of the public and competitive games [the Carnival] which are celebrated every year in that same city, and since some while ago the lord pope Martin V, of blessed memory, concerned about their poverty, conceded to them by apostolic letter, that they might scatter and distribute that burden among all the Jews living anywhere in the towns and territories of the Holy Roman Church, according to those letters which were indeed later confirmed and agreed by the lord pope Paul II, of happy memory, after certain additions had been made to them, which will be more fully detailed below. And, seeing that it has recently been suggested to us on [these Jews'] behalf that this [Roman] community should send its representatives to the aforementioned provinces, cities and towns, to publish these things, and that they should demand and raise this money from the [Jewish community] in each place, and that you should distribute and assign [it] in order to cover their [general] contributions for the coming year and also the [carnival] games, which will shortly be held, as well as the rest [of that owed] from previous years, by those who did not fully pay their apportionments for those years. Also, we understand that, if the other communities ceased to pay the aforesaid contributions, this same Roman community would be unable, by any [new arrangement], to meet the aforesaid expense, with [consequent] damage to the people of Rome.

48. Life in the Roman Jewry, c. 1520

A description of the life and activities of the Jewish community in Rome, just after Martin Luther had pinned up his ninety-five theses and shortly before the sack of the city by Imperial troops in 1527. The writer is a Spanish priest, who recounts a fictional conversation between the Lozana [a name variously translated as 'lively', 'haughty' or 'lusty'], a Spanish *conversa* from Córdoba and the 'heroine' of the work, and her young companion Rampín, with whom she had slept the previous night and who was henceforth to be her servant. There follows a dialogue between both these characters and a Roman Jew called Trigo [lit. 'wheat', the most prized form of grain at the time]. He agrees to try to sell a diamond ring, which Rampín had stolen from his previous master. In masterly fashion, the Jew beats them down in the matter of profit. The novel is written in dialogue form, like a stage-play.

[From Francisco Delicado, *La Lozana andaluza*, ed. Bruno Damiani, Madrid, 1982, pp. 83-5; in Spanish]

Chapter Sixteen

How [the Lozana and Rampín] go into the Jewish quarter and see the synagogues.

Lozana. It smells good here, they must be getting ready for a party. By my life, it smells of roast piglet!

Rampín. Can't you see that all these people are Jews? Tomorrow is the Sabbath and they're cooking **adafina**. Look at those braziers with the cooking-pots above them.

Lozana. Yes, by your life! They're experts at cooking with charcoal. There's nothing like food that's been cooked on a charcoal fire in an earthenware pot. Tell me, what's that house which all those people are going into?

Rampín. Let's go over there and you'll see. This is the synagogue of the Catalans, and that one down there is for the women. The Germans' one is over there, and that other one is for the French, and that one is for the Romans and the Italians, who are more useless as Jews than the ones from any other nation. They try to make out they're Gentiles and don't know their Law. Our Spaniards know more than any of them, because there are university graduates and rich people among them, and they're really learned. Look at them, they're over there. How does it look to you? That woman takes the biscuit. Those two men are great friends of ours and I know their wives. They go round Rome saying prayers for people who are getting married, and fasting [in intercession] for girls, so that they'll have babies in the first year.

Lozana. I could do that better than them, any time, with melted lead. They're not going to beat me there. The Moors in the Levant taught me how to fool stupid women. I'll make them see wonders, with the white of an egg, in a glass thing like a clean urinal [used for taking medical samples], so that they can get money from other people's purses by denouncing robbers.

Rampín. If only I'd known that when some gloves were stolen from me, which I had taken from my master as my salary, they'd be yours now, because they were beautiful. His girlfriend dropped a jewel and I found it. You can see it here. He's already spent two ducats on Jews to guess where it is, and I couldn't bring myself to tell him that I had it.

Lozana. Show it to me. This is a diamond! Let's sell it. I'll say I brought it back from the Middle East.

Rampín. All right. Let's go to that Jew there, who's called Trigo. Can you see him? He's coming out from there. Let's follow him. He won't utter a word unless he's heard the word 'gold' first, because [the Jews] regard it as a good omen.

Lozana. 'All that glistens is not gold.'

Trigo. What are you saying, Genoese lady [this was the false identity adopted at the time by the Spanish woman]? 'The good Jew makes gold out of straw.' So God can't fail me, because he spoke about gold too [e.g. Isaiah 60:17: 'Instead of bronze I will bring gold'].

– And you, relative [addressed to Rampín], what are you after? Are you coming here with this lady? What does she want? Well, you know already that everything will be sorted out, because I can see from her face that she's a bit of all right. Let's go to my house. Come in.

– Tina! Tina! Come downstairs and bring a cushion here for this lady – and get something nice ready for her to eat!

Lozana. Don't prepare anything, we've already eaten.

Trigo. Do her some good, as she did to Jacob [apparently a scurrilous reference to the patriarch of Israel, Jacob son of Isaac; Genesis 25-35].

Lozana. Brother [Rampín], what shall we say to him first?

Rampín. Tell him about the stone.

Lozana. Look here, I'd like to sell this jewel.

Trigo. The one in your hand? It looks like a good, well-cut diamond.

Lozana. What might it be worth?

Trigo. I'll tell you. If any great Venetian lord was here to take it, we'd soon do a deal. And you, what price did you pay for it?

Lozana. Twenty ducats.

Trigo. You won't get that much for it, I can tell you. Stay here until tomorrow and we'll see what we can do for you. It'll be amazing if we can find anyone who'll pay ten for it.

Rampín. Look here, if you can find anyone, let them have it.

Trigo. Wait for me here. Have you got anything else in the way of jewellery?

Lozana. Not at the moment. [To Rampín] You see what a conscientious Jew he is?

Rampín. Can you see him? He's coming back.

Trigo. Madam, it's already been looked at and examined. The silversmith will only give six [ducats] for it, and if not, you'll see it back here, safe and sound, and he won't give any more. Also, he says that you ought to pay me for my trouble and for brokerage. In addition, he said I should go straight back; if I don't, he won't give a farthing for it afterwards.

Lozana. Let him give seven, and you can pay yourself from that. For my part, I'll see you all right [in the context, this probably means sexual services].

Trigo. That way, it'll cost eight.

Lozana. How's that?

Trigo. Seven for the stone, and one for me for brokerage. That would be a good price, and you shouldn't let the first offer go. Five ducats go a long way in Rome.

Lozana. How do you make it five?

Trigo. If you pay me one, you'll only be left with five. That's a Jew's profit.

Rampín. Go on, give it to him. We won't get anywhere with these Jews if they change their minds.

– Go on, Trigo, take it, and see if you can get any more for it.

Trigo. I'll do that, for love of you.

49. The Jew and the Renaissance: Italy, 1571–1600

Leon Modena describes his early years, and reveals many aspects of Jewish life in Italy during the Renaissance and the Christian Counter-Reformation.

[From *The autobiography of a seventeenth-century Venetian rabbi. Leon Modena's 'Life of Judah'*, translated and edited by Mark R. Cohen, Princeton, 1988, pp. 76-8, 79, 80-1, 82, 84-6; in Hebrew]

I received the tradition from my father, my teacher of blessed memory, that our ancestors came from France. In his house there was a family tree going back more than five hundred years, which had been found among the writings of my grandfather, the teacher [*gaon*] of blessed memory....

This family has always combined Torah with stature, riches with honour, and great wealth with charitableness... He [Rabbi Aaron, a relative of Leon] told me that, after they left France, they dwelled for a long time in Viterbo, and then came to Modena, where they acquired property and became fruitful and multiplied. Because they were the first to establish a pawnshop there and become wealthy, they took their name from that city.... The first house they acquired in Modena is still in the possession of Moses [Leon's father], and I have seen it. In some places therein is found our crest in marble, the figure of a leopard standing on its own two hind legs with a palm branch in its paw. Moses told me that [the crest] has been in our family for more than five hundred years. He also has in his possession, in writing, the privileges of all those who ruled Modena – popes, emperors, dukes and the like – who confirmed [the crest].

Apparently, in the days of Isaac, the grandfather of my revered father of blessed memory, they moved to Bologna, though they continued to keep their house and pawnshop in Modena. As for me, because I was born and grew up in Venice, and have lived in its environs, and have been in Modena only in the last ten years and but two or three times,

I sign my name in Italian, 'Leon Modena da Venezia', and not 'da Modena'. For that city has become our byname instead of our toponym, and as such you will find it in my printed Italian writings.

For that reason my grandfather, the *gaon* Rabbi Mordecai of blessed memory, who was also a great Torah scholar, also lived in Bologna. He had been ordained by the *gaons* of his city, and I now possess his certificates of ordination. Several years earlier, he had begun a work similar to the *Beit Yosef* of the *gaon* Caro of blessed memory. He also composed many rabbinic explanations, legal rulings and other treatises, most of which are in the possession of Rabbi Aaron of Modena. He was also a great, distinguished physician, having been awarded the medical diploma while Emperor Charles V was still in Bologna. At that time he was made a *Cavalier di Speron d'Oro* – Knight of the Golden Spur – by him, for thus did the Emperor do to all those who received the medical diploma while he was there, whether Christian or Jew. He was honoured by all the people of his city and was known throughout Italy.

[My grandfather] passed away at the age of fifty in the year [5]290 [1529-1530], when the mule he was riding kicked up its leg [threw him], and the other doctors in the city, out of jealousy, bribed the expert physician treating him to put poison on the bandages and kill him…. He left four male children. The eldest was my revered father Isaac of blessed memory; the second, Rabbi Solomon of blessed memory; the third, Shemaiah of blessed memory; and the fourth, Rabbi Abtalion of blessed memory, eighteen months old at this time….

Shemaiah lived in Modena and managed the pawnshop there. But he became attracted to alchemy. A certain Gentile deceived him by showing him a deceptive increase [of value]. He enticed him to take all the silver and gold from the pawnshop and brought him to a certain room, claiming that they would melt it down and and increase its value many times over. But there he thrust a sword into Shemaiah's belly, killing him, and stole all the silver and gold and ran off. This happened the night of the burning of leaven [before Passover]. The next day, people sensed that something had happened and found him and buried him. Three days later the murderer was seized with all the silver and gold – nothing was missing – and he was quartered.

My revered father of blessed memory grew up to be wise in Torah and practical matters. At the age of seventeen he began to work in the pawnshop and in commerce…. Because of the oppressive expulsion decreed by Pope Pius V in 5327 [1567], my revered father journeyed from Bologna, leaving behind his possessions – a house, a mansion and notes of credit worth thousands of gold pieces. He took what he had in hand and came to live in Ferrara.

My mother experienced great difficulty in childbirth. I was born in the breech position, my buttocks turned round facing outwards, so that calamities turned upon me even at the beginning.... My family remained in Venice [where Leon was born] for about eight months and then set out to return to Ferrara. While they were on the way to Francolin, near Ferrara, as they disembarked from the boat, I was handed over to a Gentile porter, who ran off, clasping me to his chest. When they realised that I was missing, Samson Meshullam, of blessed memory, my revered father's manager [in his pawnshop], chased after him for about two miles; he caught him and took me, giving him many fisticuffs, and brought me back to my parents....

In the year 5339 [1578-1579] the constellations began to war against us with a strong hand and an outstretched arm. In the month of Nisan [March-April 1579], at the request of Cardinal Alvise d'Este, my revered father of blessed memory was thrown into prison because of a debt of fifteen hundred *scudi* [silver coins of a similar value to ducats] that had already been repaid. He sat there for about six months, and even after his release they distrained all our money for three years at the request of Alvise Mocenigo, who was supposed to have collected it from the aforesaid cardinal. The expenditure for claims and counter-claims was great, and no-one gained, but rather everyone lost and squandered money. My mother, of blessed memory, girded her loins like a man and rode to Ferrara and to Venice in order to speak with noblemen and judges of the land. From that time on we became impoverished, for in three years that false accusation caused us damage amounting to more than eight thousand ducats, as well as much anxiety.

In the month of Nisan 5340 [March-April 1580] my revered father sent me to Ferrara, to the home of his nephew Mordecai Modena, so that I could be taught books and wisdom, and I was there for one year.... I also had a little instruction in playing an instrument, in singing, in dancing, in writing and in Latin. But on account of two of Mordecai's maidservants who hated me and embittered my life by their wickedness – may their Master forgive them – I returned home at the end of a year.

[This was only the beginning of the distinguished religious and scholarly career of Leon Modena.]

Glossary

[Words printed in **bold** at first mention in the text]

adafina Spanish word for the cooking-pot which Jews would place in a small oven, on Friday evening, the eve of the Sabbath [see below] to provide food for the next day, when cooking was forbidden.

affinity Here, a technical term for a social group with ties of feudal obligation, or financial or other contract, to a leader or lord [see 'vassal' below].

aids Direct taxation in substitution for military service, normally voted to medieval rulers by assemblies of leading subjects.

aljama Spanish word for a community of Jews or Muslims, under Christian rule.

apostasy, apostates The denial of a previously-held religious faith, and those responsible for such an action.

apostolic Actions and attributes associated with the apostles, who were the first disciples of Jesus and preachers of his message; and so, from St Peter being regarded as the first pope, used of the Papacy.

Babel Babylon, in the Akkadian language, 'the gate of God'. Refers to the tower described in Genesis 11:1-9, which, according to this account, displeased God, because of the human ambition and pride expressed in its construction, and led to the variety of languages upon earth. [See introduction]

Bachelor *Bachiller*. Spanish term for a university graduate (as in 'Bachelor of Arts').

baptism Cleansing or washing by the application of water. It was a Jewish rite [Numbers 19:7], but was only applied to converts by Christians. Initially involving immersion of adults, by the fifteenth and sixteenth centuries, the ceremony normally involved the sprinkling of babies with water.

Beelzebub A name for the prince of devils [Lit. 'the lord of the flies'], the title of a Philistine god, that is, of the non-Jewish population of the land of Israel (see 'Canaan' below). In the New Testament, Jesus is accused of doing miracles in Beelzebub's name [e.g. Matthew 9:34, 10:25].

benefice   From the Latin *beneficium*, a benefit or favour. In medieval society, the term was normally used to refer either to a grant made by a lord to an individual in return for personal service, or else to describe an established post in the Church.

blasphemy   An insult to God.

Blessed Sacrament   Customary Catholic term used to describe the communion service or Mass and, more particularly, the bread and wine consecrated by the priest during that service.

booths   Temporary houses made by Jews for the Autumn festival of the ingathering of the harvest, known as *Succot* [Leviticus 23:42]: Jews would live in these 'booths', or 'tabernacles', for the seven days of the festival.

brokers   Dealers in money or goods.

bull   A papal edict, from the medieval Latin *bulla*, a seal, referring to the way in which such documents were authenticated.

Cabala   See ' Kabbalah', below.

Canaan   Land to the west of the Jordan, promised in the Jewish Scriptures to the Israelites [Exodus 23:31].

canons   Here, decrees or laws of the Catholic Church.

'ceremony'   Here, a term used by the Inquisition [see below] to describe the rules and practices of the Torah, or Jewish Law [see below]. It was also used in Spain to refer to Islamic practices.

Chamber   Here, a royal household.

circumcision   The removal of the foreskin of a male, representing his becoming a Jew [Genesis 17:10]. Also a Muslim practice.

college   In late medieval and early modern usage, refers not only to university foundations, but also to other professional bodies, including, in certain cases, groups of priests.

commune   Originally a voluntary sworn association of individuals, together for a common purpose. In Italy in this period, the term was commonly used to refer to a city-state and its government.

conversion   A radical change of religious belief and practice, in this case generally from Judaism to Christianity.

converso   Spanish word for a convert, used to refer to Jews who became Christians.

cordovanes   Leather goods, generally of goat-skin. The name comes from Córdoba, a city noted for leather crafts.

corregidor [Portuguese: *corregedor*]   The chief royal magistrate in a Castilian or Portuguese town, with wide-ranging legal and governmental powers.

Cortes	The parliamentary assemblies of various Iberian kingdoms.
coscoja	A red dye made from the bodies of berry-shaped insects found on the evergreen kermes oak, common in southern Europe and North Africa.
Creed	Documentary statement of the beliefs of the Christian Church.
diocese	The territory under the pastoral care of a bishop.
doctors	Teachers, either of Christianity or of medicine (hence the conventional modern use of the word).
ducat	A gold coin minted in Venice, and imitated elsewhere, for example in fifteenth- and sixteenth-century Spain.
Edomite	Conventional Jewish term for a Christian. From Edom, the Biblical kingdom of the supposed descendants of Esau, the son of Isaac who, through trickery, lost his inheritance to his brother Jacob, the founder of Israel [Genesis 25, 27, 36].
Elijah	Jewish prophet who was believed by Jews and Christians to have an important part to play in the coming of the Messiah [see below]. [1 Kings 17-19; Malachi 4:5; Matthew 11:14.]
Eucharist	Christian service involving the consecration of bread and wine, as instituted by Jesus on the night in which he was betrayed and arrested [Matthew 26: 26-28]
Exchequer	The financial department of a government, named after the chequered cloth, as in a chessboard, which was used to keep royal accounts in medieval England.
Exodus	A mass departure of people, in this case of the people of Israel from Egypt, which is described in the book of the same name, in the Bible.
feast	Here a religious celebration.
Fisherman	Here referring to St Peter, one of Jesus's disciples and first bishop of Rome.
Ghemarot Talmut	See 'Talmud' below.
ghetto	A walled quarter of a city, to which Jews might be confined by law. The term originated in the site of the 'new foundry' [*ghetto nuovo*] in Venice, in which Jews were first thus confined in 1516.
goy [plural *goyim*]	Hebrew word for a non-Jew, or Gentile.
Grace	Here a Christian theological term, to describe God's mercy.
grandee	From the Spanish *grande*, a term for a leading member of the nobility.
Hail Mary	From the angel Gabriel's greeting to the Virgin Mary, announcing to her that she would bear Jesus as her son [Luke 1 26:38]. In the fifteenth and sixteenth centuries, a version of this account formed an important part of Catholic devotion.

Hebrew	In the usage of Portugal, Italy and some other European countries, a term generally used to mean Jewish.
heretic	From the Greek *haeresis*, a choice. Used in this period to denote those who rejected some or all of Catholic teaching.
Holofernes	See 'Judith', below.
Holy Office	See 'Inquisition', below.
Hussites	A group of heretics in Bohemia, followers of Jan Hus, who broke away from the Catholic Church during the fifteenth century and survive to this day as a separate Church.
immunities	Exemptions from taxes or the activities of a superior judicial authority. Such grants might be made either to groups or to individuals.
Inquisition	A specialised tribunal of the Catholic Church, with the duty of investigating the religious beliefs and practices of members of the Church.
Ishmaelite	Biblical term for the sons of Ishmael, himself a son of Abraham. [Genesis 16:15 and I Chronicles 1:29-31.] The term was used by Jews in this period to refer to Muslims.
Israelites	Biblical term for Jews.
Jewry	The Jewish quarter of a medieval town or city, whether chosen voluntarily by them or imposed upon them by Christian authorities.
Judah	One of the tribes of Israel.
'judaise'	Adherence by baptised Christians to Jewish faith and practice.
Judith	A Jewish woman who, according to the account in the book of that name, which seems to have been composed in about 100 B.C., saved her people from conquest by the Assyrian ruler Nebuchadnezzar by seducing and murdering his chief commander, Holofernes. This book, written in Greek, is included in the collection of writings which was produced between the 'Old' and 'New' Testaments of the Christian Bible, which is known as the Apocrypha. As the 'apocryphal' books were included in the Latin Bible, the Vulgate, they were familiar to Catholics in the fifteenth and sixteenth centuries.
Kabbalah [Cabala]	A form of mystical Judaism practised in the late medieval and early modern periods.
'Law'	See 'Torah', below.
Levi [Levites]	Jewish tribe which in Biblical times had priestly duties in the Temple at Jerusalem.
levirate	Jewish marriage custom in which, if a woman's husband died, and his brother was still alive, the latter was required to marry her. [Deuteronomy 25:5-10.]

liberties	Legal and economic exemptions or privileges, granted by rulers to individuals or groups.
Licentiate	Term used to describe a university graduate who had a licence to teach.
Magnificent	From the Italian *magnifico*, an honorific title meaning 'honourable' or 'mighty'.
maravedi	A unit of currency in Spain (Castile), based on an earlier coin of that name, but, by the fifteenth century, no more than a unit of account.
March	Here, a term to describe a frontier region between two states.
martyrology	A collection of names and details of Christians who died for their faith.
Mass	See 'Eucharist', above.
merino/ merindad	A royal official with territorial responsibilities in Old Castile. His area of jurisdiction was known as a *merindad*.
Messiah	Lit. 'the anointed one'. Originally the title of a king, it came to be applied to a future ruler who would restore Jewish power. The title was applied to Jesus in John's gospel [1:41; 4:25].
Messianism	The belief, commonly held among Jews, that a king would ultimately come to free them from oppression and bring them to a new kingdom in the land of Israel. Christians believe Jesus to fulfil such a role.
military orders	Religious orders of knights, who formed a military force but were also under monastic vows. They originated in the Holy Land in the twelfth century, and still had considerable wealth, and some power, in fifteenth-century Spain.
missal	Book containing texts for use in the Mass [see above].
Moors	Spanish term for Muslims, especially those of the Iberian peninsula and North Africa.
New Christian	Spanish term for a convert, or, by extension, a descendant of a convert from Judaism to Christianity.
Old Christian	A Spaniard who at least claimed not to be descended from Jews, Muslims or Christian heretics.
ordinary	Here, a churchman with general legal authority in a particular area or institution.
Our Lady	Conventional title of Mary, the mother of Jesus.
pagan	Term used in this period by the Catholic Church to denote someone who was not a Christian, a Jew or a Muslim
Passover	Jewish festival to commemorate the escape of the people of Israel from Egypt. [Exodus 34:25.]

penance The act of making amends for wrongdoing. Such acts were demanded by the medieval Church after sins had been confessed to a priest.

phylacteries Passages of Jewish scripture which were to be worn by males in leather containers on their foreheads, as a reminder of the prescriptions of the Torah [see below].

places *Lugar:* Spanish term for a small centre of population.

pogrom An organised massacre of Jews, originally in late nineteenth-century Russia. The term does not originate in medieval Europe.

Pontiff From the Latin *pontifex*, a pagan priest. A title used by medieval and early modern popes, whose reigns were therefore known as 'pontificates'.

prayer-shawl A white shawl, with black decoration, worn by male Jews during their religious devotions.

procurator fiscal Prosecuting lawyer of the Spanish Inquisition.

purgatory The place in which, according to Catholic teaching, the souls of righteous Christians were purged of their lesser (venial) sins before admission to heaven.

Pythagorean A supposed or actual follower of the Greek philosopher Pythagoras [c. 540 B.C.].

rabbi A Jewish religious teacher.

regidor A member of a town council in Castile.

requests A direct tax in Castile, voted at the request of the monarch [*pedidos*].

Rock A term commonly used in the Jewish scriptures to refer to God.

Sabbath The Jewish day of rest, a focus of religious devotion [Genesis 2:2-3].

saints Lit. 'holy ones': those Christians recognised by the Catholic Church as particularly virtuous in their lives and as having the ability to use their prayers, after death, to help other Christians.

Santa Hermandad The 'Holy Brotherhood'. An organisation set up in Castile by Ferdinand and Isabella to keep order in the countryside and raise money for their war against the Muslim kingdom of Granada [1481-1492].

Saracen Medieval Christian term for a Muslim.

scribes The writers of manuscript copies of the Jewish Law [see Torah, below].

sect Lit. a 'division': normally used to refer to a minority group, for example in Judaism or Christianity, which becomes separated from the main body.

secular arm   Term used by the Inquisition [see above] to describe the non-Church authorities to whom condemned relapsed heretics were handed over for burning.

seigneurial jurisdiction   The legal powers over people and resources which might, in medieval Europe, be delegated by a ruler to a nobleman or to the Church.

synagogue   A Jewish meeting-house for worship and study.

Talmud   Post-biblical Jewish texts which formed the basis of the religious life of late medieval and early modern European Jews.

Torah   The Biblical 'Law' given to Moses on Mount Sinai [Exodus 19–20].

Trinity   The Christian concept of God as three Persons: God the Father, Jesus the Son, and the Holy Spirit.

twentieth   A direct tax on wealth, in Italy known as the *vigesima*.

university   Used in this period to refer not only to academic institutions but to a wide range of other professional associations.

vassal   A person subjected to the lordship of another, in medieval Europe.

vicar   Lit. a 'deputy' or 'substitute': in medieval Europe normally used of a subordinate official in the Church or, on occasions, in secular government.

Vulgate   The Latin translation of the Bible, attributed to Jerome [c. 341–420], which was in common use in Catholic Europe in the Middle Ages.

Bibliography of printed works cited

Robert Alter, Frank Kermode, eds, *The literary guide to the Bible*, London, 1987.

Augustine, Saint, *The City of God*, trans. John Healey, ed. R. V. G. Tasker, 2 vols, London, 1945.

Fritz (Yitzhak) Baer, *Die Juden im christlichen Spanien*, Berlin, 1929, 1936, reprinted 1970.

Malcolm Barber, *The two cities. Medieval Europe, 1050-1320*, London, 1992.

Haim Beinart, *Trujillo. A Jewish community in Extremadura on the eve of the expulsion from Spain, Hispania Judaica*, II, Jerusalem, 1980.

Eloy Benito Ruano, *Los orígenes del problema converso*, Barcelona, 1976.

Andrés Bernáldez, *Memorias de los Reyes Católicos*, ed. M. Gómez-Moreno and J. de M. Carriazo, Madrid, 1962.

Biblia sacra iuxta vulgatam clementinam, ed. Alberto Colunga, O.P. and Laurentio Turrado, Madrid, 1977.

P. R. L. Brown, *Augustine of Hippo*, London, 1967.

Jean Calvin, *Institution de la religion Chrestienne*, ed. Jean-Daniel Benoît, Paris, 1957.

Dwayne E. Carpenter, *Alfonso X and the Jews: an edition of and commentary on 'Siete Partidas' 7: 24, 'De los judíos'*, Modern Philology, CXV, Berkeley, Los Angeles, London, 1986.

Carlos Carrete Parrondo, *El tribunal de la Inquisición en el obispado de Soria (1486-1502), Fontes Iudæorum Regni Castellæ*, II, Salamanca, 1985.

Carlos Carrete Parrondo and Carolina Fraile Conde, *Los judeoconversos de Almazán, 1501-1505. Origen familiar de los Lainez, Fontes Iudæorum Regni Castellæ, IV*, Salamanca, 1987.

William A. Christian, Jr, *Local religion in sixteenth-century Spain*, Princeton, 1981.

Jeremy Cohen, *The friars and the Jews. The evolution of medieval anti-Judaism*, Ithaca and London, 1982.

Roger Collins, *Early medieval Spain. Unity in diversity, 400-1000*, London, 1983.

Rafael Conde and Delgado de Molina, *La expulsión de los Judíos de la Corona de Aragón. Documentos para su estudio*, Zaragoza, 1991.

Elvira Cunha de Azevedo Mea, 'Oraçiones judaicas na Inquisição Portuguesa-seculo XVI', in Yosef Kaplan, ed., *Jews and Conversos. Studies in society and the Inquisition*, Jerusalem, 1985, pp. 149-78.

Francisco Delicado, *La Lozana andaluza*, ed. Bruno Damiani, Madrid, 1982.

Le dictionnaire des inquisiteurs, ed. Luis Sala-Molins, Paris and the Hague, 1978.

Eamon Duffy, *The stripping of the altars. Traditional religion in England, 1400-1580*, New Haven and London, 1992.

John Edwards, 'The *conversos*: a theological approach', *Bulletin of Hispanic Studies*, LXII, 1985, pp. 39-49.

John Edwards, 'Conversos, Judaism and the language of monarchy in fifteenth-century Castile', in Circa 1492. Proceedings of the Jerusalem Colloquium: Litteræ Judærum in Terra Hispanica, ed. Isaac Benabu, Jerusalem, 1992, pp. 207-23.

John Edwards, 'Debate. Religious faith, doubt and atheism', Past and Present, 128, 1990, pp. 158-60.

John Edwards, The Jews in Christian Europe, 1400-1700, London, 1988, rev edn 1991.

John Edwards, 'Male and female religious experience among Spanish "New Christians", 1450-1500', in The expulsion of the Jews: 1492 and after, ed. Raymond B. Waddington and Arthur Williamson, New York and London, pp. 41-51.

John Edwards, 'Religious faith and doubt in late medieval Spain: Soria circa 1450-1500', Past and Present, 120, 1988, pp. 3-25.

John Edwards, 'Why the Spanish Inquisition?', Studies in Church History, XXIX, Christianity and Judaism, 1992, pp. 221-36.

Erasmus, Collected works of, various editors, Toronto, 1974-.

Nicolau Eymerich, Le manuel de l'Inquisiteur, with additions by Luis Peña, ed. Luis Sala-Molins, Paris and The Hague, 1977.

Fidel Fita, 'La verdad sobre el martirio del Santo Niño de La Guardia, o sea el proceso y quema (16 noviembre 1491) del judío Juçe Franco de Avila', Boletín de la Real Academia de la Historia, XI, 1887, pp. 7-160.

John Gager, The origins of anti-Semitism, New York, 1983.

L. Geiger, ed., Johann Reuchlins Briefwechsel, Stuttgart, 1875.

Damião de Gois, Cronica do felicissimo Rei Don Manuel, in Damião de Gois, ed. Antonio Alvaro Doria, Lisbon, 1944.

Damião de Gois, Cronica de Don Manuel, ed. Rodrigues Lapa, in Historiadores quinhentistas, Lisbon, 1972.

Rafael Gracia Boix, Colección de documentos para la historia de la Inquisición de Córdoba, Córdoba, 1981.

Solomon Grayzel, The Church and the Jews in the thirteenth century, Philadelphia, 1933.

Bernard Gui, Le manuel de l'Inquisiteur, ed. G. Mollat, 2 vols, Paris, 1964.

Bernard Hamilton, The medieval Inquisition, London, 1981.

Sebastián de Horozco, La historia del niño inocente de La Guardia, in Jack Weiner, ed., Relaciones históricas toledanas, Toledo, 1981, pp. 29-38.

Pier Cesare Ioly Zorattini, Processi del S. Uffizio di Venezia contro Ebrei e Giudaizzanti (1548-1560), 3 vols, Florence, 1980-1984.

Jonathan Israel, European Jewry in the age of mercantilism, 1550-1750, Oxford, 1987.

William James, The varieties of religious experience, Cambridge, Mass., 1985.

Ann Jefferson and David Robey, Modern literary theory. A comparative introduction, London, 1982.

Jerusalem Bible, The, ed. Alexander Jones, London, 1968.

W. C. Jordan, The French monarchy and the Jews. From Philip Augustus to the last Capetians, Philadelphia, 1989.

Yosef Kaplan, ed., *Jews and conversos. Studies in society and the Inquisition*, Jerusalem, 1985.

Leszek Kolakowski, *Religion: if there is no God*, Glasgow, 1982.

Gavin I. Langmuir, *History, religion and Antisemitism*, Berkeley, Los Angeles and Oxford, 1990.

Gavin I. Langmuir, *Toward a definition of Antisemitism*, Berkeley, Los Angeles, Oxford, 1990.

Nicholas Lash, *Easter in ordinary. Reflections on human experience and the knowledge of God*, London, 1988.

Renée Levine [Melamed], 'Women in Spanish crypto-Judaism, 1492-1520', unpublished Ph.D. thesis, Brandeis, 1982.

Jerzy Lukowski, *Liberty's folly. The Polish Lithuanian Commonwealth in the eighteenth century*, London, 1991.

Martin Luther, *Luther's works*, vol. XLV, ed. and trans. Walther I. Brandt, Philadelphia, 1962, and vol. XLVII, ed. and trans., Franklin Sherman, Philadelphia, 1971.

Michele Luzzati, *La casa dell'Ebreo. Saggi sugli Ebrei a Pisa e in Toscana nel Medioevo e nel Rinascimento, Cultura e Storia Pisana*, 7, Pisa, 1985, pp. 49-57, and 203-34.

Hyam Maccoby, *Judaism on trial. Jewish-Christian disputations in the Middle Ages*, London and Toronto, 1982.

Eleanor McLaughlin, 'Women, power and the pursuit of holiness in medieval Christianity', in *Feminist theology. A reader*, ed. Ann Loades, London, 1990, pp. 99-123.

J. D. Mansi, *Sacrorum conciliorum nova et amplissima collectio*, Florence, 1759-1798, reprinted 1962.

Thérèse and Mendel Metzger, *Jewish life in the Middle Ages. Illuminated Hebrew manuscripts of the thirteenth to sixteenth centuries*, New York 1982.

Leon Modena, *The autobiography of a seventeenth-century Venetian rabbi. Leon Modena's 'Life of Judah'*, trans. and ed. Mark R. Cohen, Princeton, 1988.

Yolanda Moreno Koch, ed., *De iure hispano-hebraico. Las taqqanot de Valladolid de 1432. Un estatuto comunal renovador, Fontes Iudæorum Regni Castellæ*, V, Salamanca, 1987.

Colin Morris, *The Papal monarchy: the Western Church, 1050-1250*, Oxford, 1988.

Moisés Orfali Levi, *Los conversos españoles en la literatura rabínica. Problemas jurídicos y opiniones legales durante los siglos XII-XVI*, Salamanca, 1982.

Otto of Freising, *The two cities. A chronicle of universal history to the year 1146 A.D.*, trans. C. C. Mierow, New York, 1966.

Amilcar Paulo, 'O ritual dos criptojudeus portugueses (algumas reflexões sobre os seus ritos)', in Yosef Kaplan, ed., *Jews and conversos. Studies in society and the Inquisition*, Jerusalem, 1985, pp. 139-48.

Maria José Pimenta Ferro Tavares, *Judaismo e Inquisição. Estudos*, Lisbon, 1987.

Brian Pullan, *The Jews of Europe and the Inquisition of Venice, 1550-1670*, Oxford, 1983.

Johann Reuchlin, *On the art of the Kabbalah [De arte Cabalistica]*, ed. and trans.

Martin and Sarah Goodman, New York, 1983.

Ellis Rivkin, 'How Jewish were the New Christians?', in Josep M. Solà, Samuel G. Armistead and Joseph H. Silverman, eds, *Hispania Judaica: studies on the history, language and literature of the Jews in the Hispanic world*, I, *History*, Barcelona, 1980, pp. 105-15.

Ellis Rivkin, 'The utilisation of non-Jewish sources for the reconstruction of Jewish history', *Jewish Quarterly Review*, XLVIII, 1957-8, pp. 183-203.

Mark Saperstein, *Jewish preaching, 1200-1800*, New Haven and London, 1989.

Shlomo Simonsohn, *The Apostolic See and the Jews*, 8 vols, Toronto, 1988-1991.

Shlomo Simonsohn, *The Jews of the duchy of Milan*, 4 vols, Jerusalem, 1982-1986.

C. John Sommerville, 'Debate. Religious faith, doubt and atheism. Comment', *Past and Present*, 128, 1990, pp. 152-5.

George Steiner, *After Babel. Aspects of language and translation*, Oxford, 1975, 1993.

Luis Suárez Fernández, *Documentos acerca de la expulsión de los Judíos*, Valladolid, 1964.

R. N. Swanson, *Catholic England. Faith, religion and observance before the Reformation*, Manchester, 1993.

R. N. Swanson, 'Medieval liturgy as theatre: the props', *Studies in Church History*, XXIX 1992, pp. 239-53.

Carsten Peter Thiede, *Heritage of the first Christians. Tracing early Christianity in Europe*, trans. Knut Hein, Oxford, 1992.

C. R. Thompson, trans., *The Colloquies of Erasmus*, Chicago, 1965.

B. Tierney, *The crisis of Church and state, 1050-1300*, Englewood Cliffs, N.J., 1964.

Ariel Toaff, *The Jews in Umbria*, I, *1245-1435*, Leiden, 1993.

Joshua Trachtenberg, *The Devil and the Jews*, New Haven, 1943.

Walter Ullmann, *A short history of the Papacy in the Middle Ages*, London, 1972.

W. A. Wakefield, *Heresy, Crusade and Inquisition in southern France, 1100-1250*, London, 1974.

Benedicta Ward, 'Saints and sybils: Hildegard of Bingen to Teresa of Avila', in *After Eve. Women, theology and the Christian tradition*, ed. Janet Martin Soskice, London, 1990, pp. 103-18.

Index